OFFICIAL SQA PAST PAPERS WITH ANSWERS

INTERMEDIATE 2

COMPUTING
2008-2012

SQA

BrightRED
PUBLISHING

First exam published in 2008.
Published by Bright Red Publishing Ltd, 6 Stafford Street, Edinburgh EH3 7AU
tel: 0131 220 5804 fax: 0131 220 6710 info@brightredpublishing.co.uk www.brightredpublishing.co.uk

ISBN 978-1-84948-269-1

A CIP Catalogue record for this book is available from the British Library.

Bright Red Publishing is grateful to the copyright holders, as credited on the final page of the Question Section, for permission to use
their material. Every effort has been made to trace the copyright holders and to obtain their permission for the use of copyright material.
Bright Red Publishing will be happy to receive information allowing us to rectify any error or omission in future editions.

[BLANK PAGE]

X206/201

NATIONAL
QUALIFICATIONS
2008

MONDAY, 2 JUNE
9.00 AM – 10.30 AM

COMPUTING
INTERMEDIATE 2

Attempt Section I and Section II and **one** Part of Section III.

Section I – Attempt all questions.

Section II – Attempt all questions.

Section III– This section has three parts:

Part A – Artificial Intelligence

Part B – Computer Networking

Part C – Multimedia Technology

Choose **one** part and answer **all** of the questions in that part.

Read each question carefully.

Write your answers in the answer book provided. **Do not** write on the question paper.

Write as neatly as possible.

Answer in sentences wherever possible.

SECTION I

Attempt ALL questions in this section.

Marks

1. State **two** advantages of using binary numbers rather than decimal numbers in a computer system. **(2)**

2. State **one** function of a *server* on a network. **(1)**

3. A printer is connected to a computer using an *interface*. Describe **one** function of an "interface". **(1)**

4. Describe **one** use of an LCD panel on a printer. **(1)**

5. Describe **one** benefit of using a mailing list when contacting a large number of people by e-mail. **(1)**

6. Sunita can store 75 photographs on a 256 Mb memory card in her digital camera. She alters the settings and can now store 101 photographs on the same memory card. Describe the alteration she has made to the settings. **(1)**

7. Name the stages labelled **X** and **Y** which are missing from the software development process listed below:

    X
    Design
    Y
    Testing
    Documentation
    Evaluation
    Maintenance. **(2)**

8. A teacher evaluates new software and decides it carries out the tasks she wants but the menus and screen layout could be better.

    (*a*) Which **one** of the following has she **not** evaluated:

    - fitness for purpose
    - readability
    - user interface? **1**

    (*b*) Each morning the teacher has to go through a number of steps on the computer to print a list of absent pupils in alphabetical order. Describe what she could do, so that this can be done efficiently in one step. **1**

    (2)

Marks

9. A travel agent wants a program to store an alphabetical list of winter holiday destinations. State the most efficient way to store lists using a programming language. **(1)**

10. A conditional statement is used in a program to decide if a discount is given to customers buying theatre tickets.

IF day is Monday OR (age>60 AND day is NOT Saturday) then
   Discount given
ELSE
   No discount
End if

What are the expected results for the following sets of test data?

(*a*)   age = 58, day = Monday   1

(*b*)   age = 65, day = Saturday   1

            (2)

11. State **one** use for an embedded computer in the home. **(1)**

(15)

[*END OF SECTION I*]

[Turn over for Section II

SECTION II

Attempt ALL questions in this section.

Marks

12. Azam draws the diagram below to represent a computer system.

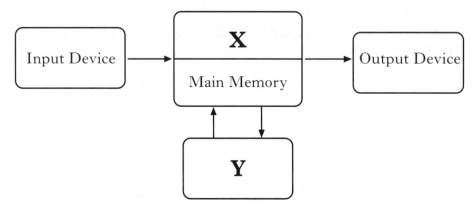

(a) The part labelled **X** contains the *Arithmetic and Logic Unit*, the *Control Unit* and the *Registers*. Name part **X**.   1

(b) Name the part labelled **Y**.   1

(c) Azam visits his local computer shop and notes down the specification of a laptop computer as shown below.

> - 2.83 GHz
> - 1 Gb RAM
> - 512 Mb ROM
> - 80 Gb hard drive
> - CD-RW drive

    (i) What is the *clock speed* of the laptop?   1

    (ii) Describe **two** differences, other than cost, between a CD-R disk and a hard disk.   2

    (iii) Azam looks at a website that advertises laptops. When he clicks on the words "Laptop Guide" another Web page opens with tips for buying laptops. Explain why this happens.   1

    (iv) Name a suitable input device that Azam should buy so that he can use his laptop for video conferencing.   1

(d) Azam designs a program that uses the formula below to convert terabytes to kilobytes.

> kilobytes = terabytes multiplied by 2^{30}

Using a high level language with which you are familiar, write the line of **code** for the formula shown above.   2

(e) Azam writes a program in a high level language and it is translated using a compiler. After successfully running the program a few times, he decides to make some changes to it.

Explain why Azam will find it difficult to edit the compiled program.   1

(10)

Marks

13. Roseanne owns a Garden Centre. She has developed a program that asks the user to enter the name and the price of a plant. The program then calculates and displays a table of prices as shown below.

> **Plant**: Geranium
>
> | **Number** | **Cost(£)** |
> |---|---|
> | 1 | 1·50 |
> | 2 | 3·00 |
> | 3 | 4·50 |
> | 4 | 6·00 |
> | 5 | 7·50 |

The design for the program is shown below with step 4 blank:

> 1 get name and price of plant
> 2 display the name of plant
> 3 display the words "Number" and "Cost (£)"
> 4
> 5   display number, number times price
> 6 end loop

(a) What should step 4 of the design be?   2

(b) What type of variable should be used to store the name of the plant?   1

(c) Pseudocode has been used to represent the design. Name **one** graphical design notation.   1

(d) After using the program for several months, Roseanne decides to improve the program by adding a new feature.

Name the stage of the software development process which is being carried out when Roseanne changes her program.   1

(e) Roseanne wants the program to check that the price entered in pounds is more than 1 but less than 4. Roseanne refines step 1 as follows:

> 1.1 ask for name of plant
> 1.2 repeat
> 1.3   ask for price of plant
> 1.4   if price <= 1 OR price>=4 then
> 1.5   display error message
> 1.6   end if
> 1.7 until _____

(i) Name the standard algorithm being used to check the price.   1

(ii) Write the condition needed to complete step 1.7.   2

(iii) Once Roseanne has coded the algorithm she tests it with the price £6. Explain why Roseanne used this test data.   1

Marks

13. (continued)

(f) Roseanne uses a database to store details of books stocked by the Garden Centre. She uses the database to produce lists of books on special offer.

List A

Title	Price
Bulbs for Spring	£8
Green Lawns	£5
Orchids	£9
Bonsai for Beginners	£3

List B

Title	Price
Orchids	£9
Bulbs for Spring	£8
Green Lawns	£5
Bonsai for Beginners	£3

Identify **one object** and **one operation** that was carried out on that object to change List A into List B.

2

(11)

Marks

14. Harry buys anti-virus software on the Internet. He downloads the software and he also downloads a *user guide* and a *technical guide* for the software.

(a) Name the stage of the software development process at which a "user guide" and a "technical guide" are produced.   **1**

(b) The format of the files for both guides is *rich text*. Explain why "rich text" is used in this situation.   **1**

(c) State the type of network to which Harry's computer is connected when he is downloading the software.   **1**

(d) Harry cannot remember where he saved the file for the user guide. He uses a program which asks him to enter the name of the file and then it finds the file for him.

Which of the following standard algorithms does the program use to find the file:

- Input validation
- Linear search
- Find maximum
- Find minimum
- Count occurrences?   **1**

(e) Once installed on Harry's computer the anti-virus icon appears on the desktop as a black and white bitmapped graphic. The graphic is 20 pixels by 64 pixels.
Calculate the storage requirements of the icon in bytes.
Show all working.   **2**

(f) When Harry runs the anti-virus software it detects a virus in the *operating system*.

(i) State **one** way in which his computer could have been infected by this virus.   **1**

(ii) What is the purpose of an "operating system"?   **1**

(g) Harry gives a copy of the anti-virus software to his brother. Name the law which Harry may have broken.   **1**

(9)

[END OF SECTION II]

[Turn over for Section III

SECTION III

Attempt ONE part of Section III

Choose **one** part and answer **all** of the questions in that part.

SECTION III

Part A—Artificial Intelligence

Marks

Attempt ALL questions in this section.

15. Newtown Hospital uses *artificial intelligence* applications for some tasks. One example is MedicTalk language processing software. This is installed on the doctors' computers to help communication with foreign patients. The doctor speaks a sentence in English, selects the required language and MedicTalk repeats it in that language.

(a) Describe **one** aspect of human intelligence, other than the ability to communicate. 1

(b) Eliza is an early example of language processing which imitates a conversation with a psychologist.

   (i) Describe **one** reason why it could be argued that Eliza **does not** show intelligence. 1

   (ii) Name the test that can be used to decide if a program is intelligent. 1

   (iii) MedicTalk has a much larger vocabulary than Eliza. Describe **one** hardware development that made this improvement possible. 1

   (iv) MedicTalk uses *speech recognition*. State **one** factor that could affect the accuracy of the "speech recognition". 1

(c) RoboCarrier is an intelligent robot used to deliver medical records within the hospital. If it meets an obstacle it stops and asks the object to move.

   (i) State how RoboCarrier could detect an obstacle in its path. 1

   (ii) As an intelligent robot, describe what RoboCarrier should do if the obstacle does not move. 1

(7)

[Turn over

Marks

16. Mr MacDonald is a fruit farmer who is using *artificial intelligence* to improve his crop production. He uses an *expert system* to select the best method of pest control.

(a) Explain what is meant by an "expert system".   1

(b) State **one** advantage of using an "expert system" rather than a human expert.   1

(c) A *vision system* is used to grade apples as perfect or damaged based on their appearance.

Describe how a "vision system" could be used to grade the apples.   2

(d) Mr MacDonald needs a loan from his bank. The bank uses an *artificial neural system* to assess the risk in giving a loan to Mr MacDonald.

    (i) Explain what is meant by an "artificial neural system".   1

    (ii) Describe **one** disadvantage of relying on an "artificial neural system".   1

(e) Mr MacDonald is using the World Wide Web to find dates and locations of Farmers' Markets in Scotland. Describe how he should use the search engine below to obtain this information.

keywords [_____] **GoFind!**

   2

   (8)

17. A travel agent requires a knowledge base about the cost of excursions. A software developer working on this project is creating a *semantic net*.

(a) Name the stage of the software development process which is being carried out.   1

(b) Draw a semantic net to represent the facts below:

Venice is a full day trip
Florence is a full day trip
The price of a full day trip is £32   2

   (3)

Marks

18. The solar ultraviolet index (UV index) can be used as a guide to the risk of skin damage from the sun. The knowledge base below shows facts about a UV index forecast for British towns and rules about the level of risk of skin damage.

    1 uv_index(blackpool, 2).
    2 uv_index(london, 5).
    3 uv_index(edinburgh, 3).
    4 uv_index(inverness, 4).
    5 uv_index(oban, 5).

    6 high_risk(X) if uv_index(X,Y) and Y>4.

    7 medium_risk(X) if uv_index(X,Y) and Y=4.

    8 medium_risk(X) if uv_index(X,Y) and Y=3.

(*a*) What would be the result of the following query:

? uv_index(london, 5).   **1**

(*b*) What would be the **first** solution to:

? medium_risk(X).   **1**

(*c*) Using the numbering system to help you, trace how the system evaluates the query:

? high_risk(oban).   **3**

(*d*) A UV index below 3 is regarded as low risk.

Use this information to complete the following rule:

low_risk(X)   **2**

      (7)

[*END OF SECTION III—PART A—ARTIFICIAL INTELLIGENCE*]

SECTION III

Part B—Computer Networking

Attempt ALL questions in this section.

Marks

19. Emiko has purchased a laptop computer.

(a) When Emiko switches on her laptop, it asks if she wants to connect to a wireless LAN (WLAN). Emiko does not have a WLAN but her neighbour does.

  (i) Name the type of transmission that her neighbour's network is using.

1

  (ii) Emiko tries to connect to the WLAN. Which part of her neighbour's wireless network hardware is Emiko communicating with?

1

  (iii) Emiko was unable to connect to her neighbour's WLAN because of *software security*.

  Describe **one** method of implementing "software security".

1

(b) Emiko e-mails her friends once a week. She writes her e-mails off-line then connects to the Internet and sends her e-mails.

  (i) Explain why Emiko writes her e-mails off-line.

1

  (ii) Name the type of Internet connection Emiko is most likely to have.

1

(c) Emiko uses a computer at work to send the following e-mail to one of her friends.

To:	charlesyounger@xyz.org
From:	emiko@warmmail.com
Subject:	Video Clip
File(s)	Slipping on a banana.mpg (300Mb)

Hi,
Not sure if you will be interested in this video clip but I thought it was quite funny.

Emiko

  (i) Describe how sending this e-mail may have broken the code of conduct concerning the use of Networks and the Internet at her workplace.

1

  (ii) By looking at Charles Younger's e-mail address, suggest the type of organisation that he works for.

1

  (iii) Name the term used to describe a file that is included as part of an e-mail.

1

Marks

20. Rachel is a mother of two young children. She works from her home in Livingston and uses the Internet for both business and pleasure. Her two children also use the computer for Internet access.

(a) Rachel and her children use a search engine to find information.

```
keywords [_____]   [ Search ]
```

    (i) Describe how Rachel would use the search engine to get information on tennis clubs in Livingston.　　**2**

    (ii) Sometimes when the children are using the search engine they get the message "content blocked".

    Describe **one** reason why this message appeared.　　**1**

    (iii) Rachel contacts her ISP to find out why some searches have been blocked. What do the letters ISP stand for?　　**1**

(b) Rachel has written an *encryption* computer program which she is going to sell from her website.

    (i) Describe the purpose of an "encryption" program.　　**1**

    (ii) The Government has told Rachel that she must give them a copy of the key to her encryption program.

    Name the law which states that Rachel should give them a copy of the key.　　**1**

    (iii) Describe **one** economic implication of deciding to sell the program using her website rather than from a shop.　　**1**

(c) One customer has contacted Rachel and asked if he could have a *user guide* for the encryption program. Rachel replied that he can download it from:

http://www.sekrets.com/encrypt/downloads/manual.dok

    (i) When the customer enters the URL into his browser, the file is found on the server and downloaded.

    Describe how the file is found.　　**2**

    (ii) What is the pathname of the "user guide" in the URL above?　　**1**

    (iii) Describe the purpose of a "user guide".　　**1**

(d) Rachel is concerned that she might lose all the information on her computer, so she copies all her files onto a DVD-RW.

Describe **two** further actions that should be part of Rachel's backup strategy.　　**2**

(13)

Marks

21. Horst has recently returned home from hospital where he had a heart monitor fitted. This monitor will measure his heart rate and send the information to his palmtop computer.

(*a*) Name the type of communication network described above.   1

(*b*) When the heart monitor is communicating with the palmtop computer, the analogue signal from the monitor must be converted into a digital signal that the computer can understand.

Name the part of the computer that converts the analogue signal into a digital signal.   1

(*c*) If his heart rate gets too high, Horst may need medical treatment.

Describe a suitable use for converging technologies in this situation.   1

(*d*) Horst notices a "signal failure" message on his palmtop.

Name the threat to the network that has occurred.   1

(4)

[END OF SECTION III—PART B—COMPUTER NETWORKING]

SECTION III

Part C—Multimedia Technology

Marks

Attempt ALL questions in this section.

22. Andrew is a photographer who would like to sell his photographs on the World Wide Web.

    (a) When Andrew takes a photograph with his digital camera, the light passes through the lens onto the CCD.

    Explain the purpose of the CCD in a digital camera.   **1**

    (b) Andrew produces a plan on paper for the Web page that will display his photographs.

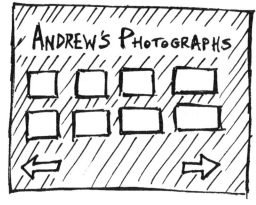

    (i) Name the stage of the software development process which Andrew is carrying out.   **1**

    (ii) Each photograph takes up 29360128 bits of memory.

    Calculate how many megabytes of memory are equal to 29360128 bits. **Show all working**.   **2**

    (c) Andrew could either use a WYSIWYG editor or a text editor to create his Web page.

    (i) Describe how a WYSIWYG editor would be used to create the Web page.   **1**

    (ii) Describe how a text editor would be used to create the Web page.   **1**

    (d) Andrew adds a button saved in GIF format to the Web page. He finds that an outline of the button appears.

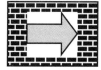

    He alters the graphic of the button so that he is able to see through the graphic to the background.

    Name the feature of a GIF graphic which allows the background to be seen.   **1**

    (e) Some customers complain that Andrew's Web page is very slow to load over their Internet connection.

    Describe **one** alteration Andrew could make to the photographs that would allow faster loading of the Web page.   **1**

    (8)

Marks

23. DigiPhones is developing a video telephone system that allows users to see and hear the person phoning them.

(a) Apart from a digital video camera, name **one** other piece of multimedia input hardware the video telephone system would require.   1

(b) DigiPhones is unsure whether to use *synthesised sound data* or *digitised sound data* when capturing the user's voice.

    (i) Explain why "synthesised sound data" would be unsuitable for this purpose.   1

    (ii) When digitising sound, one of the factors affecting *sound quality* is the *sampling rate*. Describe the relationship between the "sampling rate" and the "sound quality".   1

(c) MP3 files use *lossy compression* to reduce the amount of memory used.

    (i) Describe how "lossy compression" reduces the filesize.   1

    (ii) Name **one** uncompressed sound file format.   1

(d) When testing the video telephone system, several people complained that the *resolution* of the video was poor.

    (i) Describe what is meant by the term "resolution".   1

    (ii) Apart from altering the "resolution", describe **two** ways in which the video quality could be improved.   2

(e) DigiPhones would like to create a new ringtone.

    (i) Describe how DigiPhones could **create** the music for a new ringtone and store it on the computer without using a microphone.   1

    (ii) The ringtone is tested on the computer and heard through a loudspeaker. Apart from a loudspeaker, what other hardware would be required to output the ringtone?   1

(f) Name the correct term used to describe a mobile phone that integrates the functionality of a palmtop computer.   1

(11)

Marks

24. The image shown below was created using a graphics package.

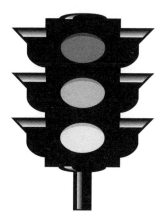

(*a*) Describe **two** methods you could use to decide if the above graphic was created in a vector graphics package or a bit-mapped graphics package.   2

(*b*) The graphic was saved using the SVG file type.

State what the letters SVG stand for.   1

(*c*) Describe how a vector graphic file stores information about each object in the graphic.   1

(*d*) From the graphic shown above, identify **one** object and **one** operation that may have been carried out on that object.   2

     (6)

[END OF SECTION III—PART C—MULTIMEDIA TECHNOLOGY]

[END OF QUESTION PAPER]

[BLANK PAGE]

[BLANK PAGE]

X206/201

NATIONAL
QUALIFICATIONS
2009

THURSDAY, 4 JUNE
9.00 AM – 10.30 AM

COMPUTING
INTERMEDIATE 2

Attempt Section I and Section II and **one** Part of Section III.

Section I – Attempt all questions.

Section II – Attempt all questions.

Section III– This section has three parts:

        Part A – Artificial Intelligence

        Part B – Computer Networking

        Part C – Multimedia Technology

Choose **one** part and answer **all** of the questions in that part.

Read each question carefully.

Write your answers in the answer book provided. **Do not** write on the question paper.

Write as neatly as possible.

Answer in sentences wherever possible.

SECTION I

Attempt ALL questions in this section.

Marks

1. State **one** benefit of networking computers.   **(1)**

2. Explain the difference between storing data in RAM and storing data on backing storage.   **(1)**

3. Name the part of the processor responsible for carrying out calculations.   **(1)**

4. Name the software that controls the process of saving files to disk.   **(1)**

5. Name **one** optical storage medium that allows the user to save files but **not** delete them.   **(1)**

6. Name an input device which is built into a palmtop computer.   **(1)**

7. Each character on the keyboard has its own ASCII code. The ASCII code for one of the *control characters* is 13.

   (*a*) Convert the decimal number 13 into a binary number.   **1**

   (*b*) Describe the function of "control characters".   **1**

   (2)

8. Explain the purpose of the *analysis* stage in the software development process.   **(1)**

9. State **one** advantage of writing programs in a high level language rather than in machine code.   **(1)**

10. Name the stage of the software development process at which the *user interface* is created.   **(1)**

11. Complete the following *complex condition* that displays a message "Slow Down" for cars whose speed is over 30, but below 35.

    IF _____ THEN display "Slow Down".   **(2)**

Marks

12. A hospital uses a program to store the length of time each person waits to see a doctor. The program reports the longest waiting time.

State which **one** of the following standard algorithms the program would use:

- Input validation
- Find maximum
- Find minimum
- Count occurrences
- Linear search **(1)**

13. Name the type of loop that a program would use to implement an *input validation* algorithm. **(1)**

(15)

[END OF SECTION I]

[Turn over for Section II

SECTION II

Attempt ALL questions in this section.

Marks

14. Marek is writing a program to calculate the average weekly rainfall.

The design for this program can be represented as follows:

```
1.   set total to zero
2.   loop 7 times
3.       get day's rainfall from user
4.       add rainfall to total
5.   end loop
6.   calculate average rainfall
7.   display average rainfall
```

(*a*)   (i)   Name the design notation that has been used above.   1

     (ii)   Name and describe a **graphical** design notation.   2

(*b*)   Steps 2 and 5 are the beginning and the end of a *fixed loop*.

Explain why a "fixed loop" is being used here.   1

(*c*)   Marek uses an *editor* at the implementation stage of the software development process.

     (i)   State the purpose of an "editor" at the implementation stage.   1

     (ii)   State where the program is stored before it is saved to backing storage.   1

(*d*)   Describe **two** methods that Marek could use to ensure that his code is *readable*.   2

(*e*)   The program calculates the average rainfall for one week as 18·6 mm.

Describe how *floating point representation* is used to represent real numbers.   2

(10)

Marks

15. The estate agent PropertyPlus has a catalogue of local properties for sale. A sample page from the catalogue is shown below.

PropertyPlus

Price	£120,000
Location	East Kirkness
Rooms	2 bedrooms, living room, family kitchen, dining room, bathroom
Garden	Front and rear garden
Parking	Off street parking

Property 1 of 65

FOR SALE FOR SALE

(a) From this sample page, identify **one** object and **one** operation that may have been carried out on the object.   2

(b) The image of the house measures 3 inches by 4 inches and has a resolution of 600 dpi.

Calculate the storage requirements for the photograph in **kilobytes**. **Show all working**.   3

(c) The photograph was taken using a digital camera. The camera was connected to a computer system through an *interface*.

State **one** function of an "interface".   1

(d) State **one** reason why the estate agent might choose a laser printer rather than an inkjet printer to print the catalogue.   1

(e) PropertyPlus makes its catalogue available on-line.

    (i) Name the type of software that is required to access this catalogue on-line.   1

    (ii) State an appropriate type of software for protecting a computer system while accessing the Internet.   1

(f) Name the legislation that requires PropertyPlus to protect information held on customers.   1

           (10)

[Turn over

Marks

16. Jenna writes a program that will calculate the speed of a car.

The algorithm for the program is shown below.

---

1. Take in distance travelled by car

2. Take in the time taken to travel this distance

3. Calculate the speed of the car

4. Display the speed of the car

(a) State **one** appropriate data type for the variables used in the program.   1

(b) The distance travelled by the car must be under 80 km.

   (i) Name the standard algorithm that should be used in this program to ensure that the distance entered is within range.   1

   (ii) Jenna tests her finished program by using 30 and 40 as examples of *normal* test data for the distance. Suggest **two** numbers that Jenna should use for *exceptional* test data.   2

(c) Jenna used an *interpreter* while developing her program. State **one** advantage of using an interpreter rather than a compiler.   1

(d) The finished program requires 84 Mb of memory.

Name the item of *documentation* that should contain this information.   1

(e) Jenna checks to see if her program is *fit for purpose*.

   (i) Name the stage of the software development process that Jenna is carrying out.   1

   (ii) State what is meant by the term "fit for purpose".   1

(f) Computer viruses pose a serious threat to computer systems.

   (i) State **one** way of spreading computer viruses.   1

   (ii) Describe **one** common symptom of a computer virus.   1

(10)

[END OF SECTION II]

SECTION III

Attempt ONE part of Section III

Choose **one** part and answer **all** of the questions in that part.

[Turn over

Marks

SECTION III

Part A—Artificial Intelligence

Attempt ALL questions in this section.

17. (a) Early artificial intelligence focused on games like noughts and crosses, draughts and chess.

    (i) State **one** reason why game playing was one of the first areas of artificial intelligence research.   1

    (ii) Name and describe the test that is used to determine whether a computer shows intelligence.   2

(b) ELIZA is a program that simulates a conversation.

    (i) Describe how ELIZA responds to input from the user.   1

    (ii) Name the **type** of program used to hold a conversation with a human.   1

(c) The Post Office uses an *artificial neural system* in the sorting office.

    Describe a task that an "artificial neural system" is used for in this situation.   1

(d) Braeness International Airport uses an intelligent robot to carry luggage.

    (i) Describe how the robot could find its way from one location in the airport to another location in the airport.   1

    (ii) State **one** advantage of using an intelligent robot to carry luggage around the airport rather than using a robot with no intelligence.   1

(e) State **one** development in computer hardware that has made progress in the field of artificial intelligence possible.   1

(9)

Marks

18. The organisation Health4Scotland has an expert system on its website to help patients plan a programme of exercise and healthy eating.

(*a*) State **two** advantages to the patient of using the expert system rather than visiting the doctor.

2

(*b*) Suggest **one** concern that doctors might have about the introduction of this expert system.

1

(*c*) Patients are able to use palmtop computers to input data into the expert system using speech recognition.

    (i) State **one** task the user will need to carry out before the speech recognition software can operate effectively.

1

    (ii) Name **one** problem that could affect the accuracy of the speech recognition system.

1

    (iii) Apart from speech recognition, name an application of artificial intelligence that could be used to input the data.

1

(6)

[Turn over

Marks

19. Xtreme Biking is a company that offers mountain biking courses. The knowledge base below holds facts and rules, and is able to match students to courses.

1 fitness(jessica, excellent).

2 fitness(shabir, excellent).

3 fitness(mary, excellent).

4 fitness(dominik, good).

5 fitness(graeme, poor).

6 owns(shabir, bike).

7 owns(graeme, bike).

8 owns(mary, bike).

9 experienced(dominik).

10 attend_intermediate_course(X) if

    experienced(X).

11 attend_advanced_course(X) if

    fitness(X excellent) and owns(X bike).

(*a*) (i) State the result of the following query:

            ? fitness(mary, good).   1

       (ii) State the result of the following query:

            ? attend_intermediate_course(X).   1

(*b*) Using the numbering system to help you, *trace* how the system will evaluate the query:

            ? attend_advanced_course(X).

       as far as the first solution.   4

                                                                    (6)

Marks

20. (*a*) A problem is represented using the search tree below.

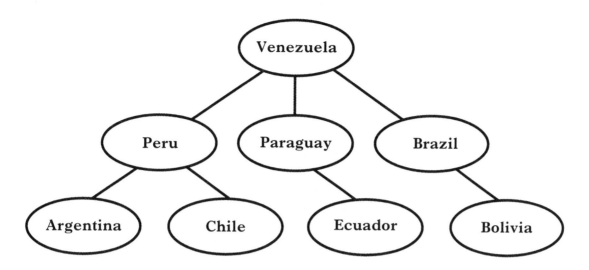

The solution to the problem is Chile.

List the nodes, in the order in which they will be visited, to reach the solution using a *breadth-first search*.   1

(*b*) One way of representing information before creating a knowledge base is by using a *semantic net*.

(i) Name the stage of the software development process at which a "semantic net" will be drawn.   1

(ii) Draw a "semantic net" to illustrate the following information:

Finland is in Northern Europe and uses the Euro as its currency.   2

(4)

[END OF SECTION III□ PART A□ ARTIFICIAL INTELLIGENCE]

SECTION III

Part B—Computer Networking

Marks

Attempt ALL questions in this section.

21. Simon has a villa which he rents to holidaymakers. He creates a website to advertise the villa. Simon chooses an ISP to host his website.
The structure of his website is shown below.

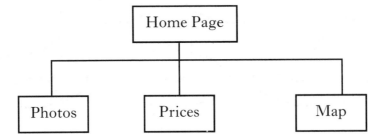

(a) State what Simon should have on his home page to help users navigate his website.

1

(b) Simon uploads his website files to the ISP host computer.

  (i) State what ISP means.

1

  (ii) Name the Internet service that Simon uses to upload his website files.

1

  (iii) Name the type of *data transmission* that Simon uses when he uploads his website files to the host computer.

1

(c) The URL for the Web page which has a map is:

http://www.isp4scots.co.uk/simonsvilla/map.html

  (i) State the domain name for this Web page.

1

  (ii) Describe the function of the *Domain Name Service*.

2

(d) Simon registers details of his website with a search engine company.

State **one** reason why this will benefit Simon.

1

(8)

Marks

22. Grange Bank uses the Internet to recruit employees. People seeking employment can fill in application forms and sit selection tests on-line. They are informed by e-mail if they are to be invited to attend for interview.

(*a*) Describe **one** cost to the bank of using the Internet to recruit staff. 1

(*b*) The bank has a version of their website formatted for mobile phones.

Name the software that will be needed to view a website on a mobile phone. 1

(*c*) Data submitted to the bank is *encrypted* and stored on disk.

Describe a situation where the bank must allow outside agencies access to "encrypted" data. 1

(*d*) An employee at a rival bank gains unauthorised access to the bank's computer and deletes some files.

(i) Name the law that the employee is breaking. 1

(ii) Describe **two** features of a *backup strategy* that would allow the bank to recover this data. 2

(*e*) Yasmina is applying for a job with the bank. She has been on-line all morning completing the application form and sitting on-line tests.

(i) State **two** reasons why an *ADSL Internet connection* is better than connecting with a *dial-up modem* in this situation. 2

(ii) Yasmina receives an e-mail inviting her to attend for interview.

The e-mail address is:

recruitment@grangebank.com

State the user name in this e-mail address. 1

(*f*) Yasmina is successful at her interview and is appointed as a financial adviser who visits customers in their own homes. She will use her laptop and a printer to form a WPAN.

(i) State what WPAN stands for. 1

(ii) Yasmina decides to use her laptop to do some on-line shopping.

Describe what the bank could do to prevent her accessing on-line shopping websites. 1

(11)

[Turn over

Marks

23. Swirlclean is a company that sells washing machines from its website. Sophie buys a washing machine from the Swirlclean website.

(*a*) Describe **one** advantage to the customers of e-sales.   1

(*b*) Sophie's washing machine is model WM07. A fault code F31 is displayed on an LCD panel on the front of the washing machine.

(i) State what LCD stands for.   1

(ii) Sophie logs onto the company's website.

Describe how she could use the screen below to get information about the fault.

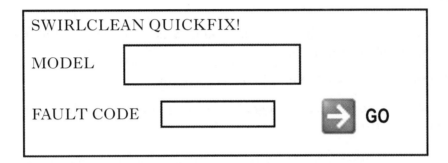

2

(*c*) Sophie phones an engineer who visits her home. He connects his laptop to the washing machine and re-installs the control software.

(i) Name the type of computer that is built in to the washing machine.   1

(ii) Describe **one** way in which *convergent technology* would have been of benefit in this situation.   1

(6)

[END OF SECTION III, PART B, COMPUTER NETWORKING]

[Turn over for Section III Part C – Multimedia Technology]

SECTION III

Part C—Multimedia Technology

Marks

Attempt ALL questions in this section.

24. Rowan High School is moving to a new building in 2010. The pupils are creating a DVD that tells the history of the school.

   (a) Mr Alexander, a previous headteacher, now lives in Canada.

   Name the input device that Mr Alexander could use so that a filmed interview with him could be captured across the Internet.   **1**

   (b) The pupils use a scanner to capture graphics from old photographs of staff and pupils.

   (i) When the photographs are scanned, reflected light is turned into an analogue signal and then digitised.

   Name the device in the scanner that does the digitising.   **1**

   (ii) The scanner software asks the user to select the *colour depth* and the *resolution*.

   A) Explain what is meant by "colour depth".   **1**

   B) Explain what is meant by "resolution".   **1**

   (iii) One of the photographs is to be altered so that only the head and shoulders show.

   Name the image editing tool that could be used to do this.   **1**

   (iv) The scanned photographs are stored as bitmap files rather than JPEG files.

   Describe the effect this will have on file size.   **1**

Marks

24. (continued)

(c) Background music for the DVD is created from a recording of the school choir. The sound wave is shown below.

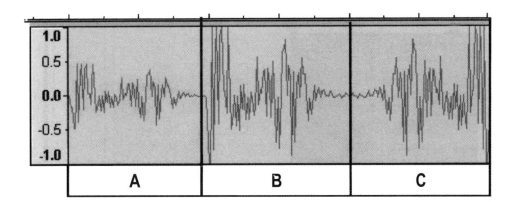

(i) Section A was copied and edited to create section B.

Name the editing feature that has been used to create section B.   **1**

(ii) Section B was copied and edited to create section C.

Name the editing feature that has been used to create section C.   **1**

(iii) Apart from speakers, name the hardware that is needed to output sound.   **1**

(d) The architects have produced a *virtual reality* guide to the new school building.

(i) Explain why the "virtual reality" application lets pupils experience the new building more fully than a slide show presentation would.   **1**

(ii) Name a file type that could be used to store the vector graphics used in the virtual reality guide.   **1**

(iii) Name **one** type of software the school could use to view a multimedia application.   **1**

(12)

[Turn over

Marks

25. Martyn produces a website that provides information for visitors to Venice. One page of the website is shown below:

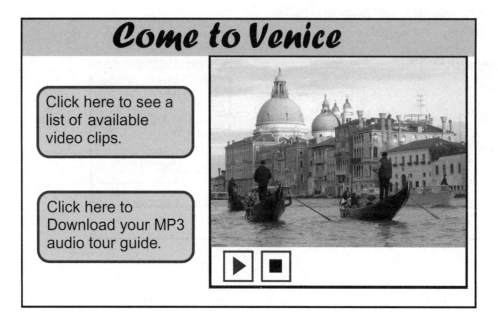

(a) When the video clips were first captured they filled the whole screen.

What change has been made to the video clip so that the whole clip can be viewed in the window shown above?   1

(b) The file size of the video clips is very large. It is reduced by decreasing the frame rate.

    (i) State **one advantage** of decreasing the frame rate rather than decreasing the video time.   1

    (ii) State **one disadvantage** of decreasing the frame rate rather than decreasing video time.   1

(c) Visitors can download an MP3 audio tour guide which they can listen to while exploring Venice.

    (i) Name the type of compression used by MP3.   1

    (ii) State **two** reasons why it is important that the audio tour files have a small size.   2

(d) Martyn is a good keyboard player. He wants to create the sounds of guitars and violins as background music for the video clips.

Name the input device he should use to create the music.   1

(e) Martyn adds more information to his website after it has been on-line for a few weeks.

Name the stage of the software development process that is being carried out.   1

(8)

Marks

26. Krysia has created a chess game using 3D graphics.

(a) Name the *attribute* of the image of a chess piece which can be changed so that the chess piece looks like wood.   **1**

(b) Krysia is creating the CD cover for the chess game. She has used graphics packages to create images of the chessboard and chess pieces as shown below.

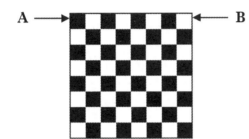 

    (i) Krysia has used a *vector graphics package to* create the chessboard.

       State **two** *attributes* that are different between square **A** and square **B** in the graphic above.   **2**

    (ii) Explain how you could prove that the graphic of the chess pieces has been produced using a *bit mapped graphics package* rather than a *vector graphics package*.   **1**

    (iii) Krysia wants the chessboard to show through the background in the graphic of the chess pieces as shown below.

       State the *attribute* of the graphic of the chess pieces that she should change to do this.   **1**

                                                               (5)

[END OF SECTION III□ PART C□ MULTIMEDIA TECHNOLOGY]

[END OF QUESTION PAPER]

[BLANK PAGE]

2010

[BLANK PAGE]

X206/201

| NATIONAL QUALIFICATIONS 2010 | THURSDAY, 3 JUNE 9.00 AM – 10.30 AM | COMPUTING INTERMEDIATE 2 |

Attempt Section I and Section II and **one** Part of Section III.

Section I – Attempt all questions.

Section II – Attempt all questions.

Section III– This section has three parts:

> Part A – Artificial Intelligence
> Part B – Computer Networking
> Part C – Multimedia Technology

Choose **one** part and answer **all** of the questions in that part.

Read each question carefully.

Write your answers in the answer book provided. **Do not** write on the question paper.

Write as neatly as possible.

Answer in sentences wherever possible.

Marks

SECTION I

Attempt ALL questions in this section.

1. Name a code that is used to represent text in a computer system.   1

2. State which type of computer system would be used by a bank to process large amounts of data at high speed.   1

3. Name the part of the processor that carries out calculations.   1

4. Jane saves her geography report at home using a *standard file format*.

   State **one** standard file format suitable for saving word processed files.   1

5. Nile Books is upgrading the computer network in its warehouse.

   (*a*) Name this type of computer network.   1

   (*b*) State **one** reason why fibre-optic cable may be used as the *transmission medium*.   1

6. State **one** reason why an *interface* is needed between the processor and a peripheral device.   1

7. High level languages are translated into machine code using an *interpreter* or a *compiler*.

   Describe **one** difference between an interpreter and a compiler.   1

8. A school is having a sponsored walk to raise money for charity. State which **one** of the following algorithms would be used to find the pupil who raised the most money:

   - Input validation
   - Linear search
   - Find maximum
   - Find minimum
   - Count occurrences.   1

9. Orla uses *pre-defined functions* in her program code.

   (*a*) State what is meant by the term "pre-defined function".   1

   (*b*) Give **one** example of a pre-defined function.   1

Marks

10. Software is evaluated in terms of *fitness for purpose*.

State what is meant by the term "fitness for purpose".   **1**

11. A *structure diagram* is used to design a solution to a programming problem.

Name and describe **one** other design notation that could be used to design a solution to a programming problem.   **2**

12. A program stores pupils' contact details. State a suitable data type for storing the postcode EH22 1LE.   **1**

    (15)

[*END OF SECTION I*]

[Turn over for Section II

Marks

SECTION II

Attempt ALL questions in this section.

13. Oro Computers is a company that assembles computer systems according to customer specifications. Some of the options available are shown below.

PROCESSOR	RAM	BACKING STORE	
2·4 GHz 2·6 GHz 3·8 GHz	1 Gb 2 Gb 4 Gb	250 Gb Hard drive 500 Gb Hard drive CD-RW drive DVD-RW drive	
NUMBER OF USB INTERFACES	**SOFTWARE**		
2 5	Graphics package requires Word processor requires Operating System requires Expel anti-virus requires	400 Mb RAM 150 Mb RAM 512 Mb RAM 512 Mb RAM	

(a) State the **fastest** *clock speed* shown above.　　　　　　　　　　　　　　　　1

(b) A customer chooses 2 Gb RAM. He also buys the *operating system* and the *anti-virus program* listed above.

　　(i) If both these programs are stored in RAM at the same time, how much RAM is available for other programs?　　　1

　　(ii) State **two** functions of an operating system.　　　2

　　(iii) State the law that is broken by deliberately sending a virus.　　　1

(c) A customer buys a computer system with 5 USB interfaces.

　　Suggest **one** reason why he wants 5 interfaces rather than 2 interfaces.　　　1

(d) State a task that may require a DVD-RW drive rather than a CD-RW drive.　　　1

(e) Apart from a hard drive, state **one** magnetic storage device that would be suitable for storing a backup copy of a 40 Mb file.　　　1

Marks

13. (continued)

(f)   The company will deliver to addresses within a distance of between 15 miles and 60 miles inclusive from the warehouse.

(i)   The Test Data Table below is not complete.

Type	Test data	Expected result
	19	Can deliver
Extreme		Can deliver
Exceptional	75	

A → (points to first Type cell)

B → (points to Extreme Test data cell)

C → (points to Exceptional Expected result cell)

State what is missing from the table at A, B and C.   3

(ii) Create the *complex condition* missing from the conditional statement below.

IF _____ then display Can Deliver   2

(13)

[Turn over

Marks

14. Pupils and staff at Sabio High School are planning a "Get Fit" campaign and have produced the following logo.

(a) Pupils used a graphics package to produce the logo.

Identify **one** *object* and **one** *operation* that may have been carried out on that object.   2

(b) Allan uses an electronic sewing machine to attach the logos to T-shirts.

(i) State the type of computer that is built into the sewing machine.   1

(ii) State **one** suitable output device that could warn Allan of an error when he starts to sew.   1

(c) Pupils write a computer program that can calculate a person's Body Mass Index (BMI) from their height in metres and weight in kilograms.

Example:

Height	1·67
Weight	58·9
BMI	21·1

(i) State the type of variable that should be used to store the weight.   1

(ii) Using a programming language with which you are familiar, write code for the formula: 2

BMI = weight divided by (height)^2

(iii) Describe **one** way to make a program *readable*.   1

(iv) Describe why poor *readability* in a program affects the *maintenance* of the program.   1

(d) The school website gives access to information on the "Get Fit" campaign. Parents can also receive updates by e-mail.

(i) Describe the most efficient way for the school to send the latest update to all the parents by e-mail.   1

(ii) State **one** way of directing people from the school website to other websites for further information.   1

(iii) State the law that may make it illegal for the school to give the parents' e-mail addresses to companies who sell fitness equipment.   1

(12)

Marks

15. One hundred runners are taking part in a charity fun race.

Companies can sponsor individual runners.

There are three levels of sponsorship:

Bronze – £50
Silver – £100
Gold   – £200

A program to process donations is being developed.

Two different versions of the user interface have been designed. These are shown below.

Interface A   **Interface B**

(a) State **two** reasons why Interface B is a more user-friendly interface than Interface A.   2

(b) Only Interface A will need to use an *input validation* algorithm when donations are entered.

   (i)   Explain why input validation will be needed with Interface A.   1

   (ii) Explain why input validation is **not** required with Interface B.   1

(c) State the data structure that should be used to store the one hundred runners' names.   1

(5)

[END OF SECTION II]

[Turn over

[BLANK PAGE]

SECTION III

Attempt ONE part of Section III

Choose **one** part and answer **all** of the questions in that part.

[Turn over

Marks

SECTION III

Part A—Artificial Intelligence

Attempt ALL questions in this section.

16. (*a*) Mateusz wants to invest money by buying shares in a company. He uses an *Artificial Neural System* to help decide which shares to purchase.

    (i)   Describe what is meant by an "Artificial Neural System".   1

    (ii)   Explain why an Artificial Neural System is used in the stock market.   1

    (iii)   State **one** other use of an Artificial Neural System.   1

(*b*) Mateusz is advised to buy shares in Intellicombat who make multi-player computer games that use artificial intelligence.

    (i)   State **one** aspect of human intelligence that artificial intelligence applications aim to copy.   1

    (ii)   In a game that shows intelligent behaviour, describe what should happen to the abilities of the characters as the game progresses.   1

    (iii)   Name the type of network to which a player must be connected in order to play against a person in another country.   1

    (6)

Marks

17. Serena has a palmtop computer. The software installed includes a diary, e-mail and *speech recognition* software. The palmtop also has a *chatterbot* facility.

(*a*) Describe **one** example of a **command** that Serena may issue when e-mailing using speech recognition. 1

(*b*) Serena would like to use *handwriting recognition* software to enter text.

State the input device that her palmtop must have for this to be possible. 1

(*c*) A chatterbot is a current example of *language processing*.

State **one** early example of a program that used language processing. 1

(*d*) Describe **one** way that a chatterbot could help Serena to be organised at the start of her working day. 1

(4)

[Turn over

Marks

18.   Scotia Forest has a large plantation of trees. Part of the forest was flooded to create a reservoir that is 250 metres deep.

(*a*)   The owners of the forest want to remove trees from under the water.

Describe **one** advantage of using *intelligent robots* for this task rather than robots with no intelligence.   **1**

(*b*)   The owners of the forest use *satellite photo interpretation* to monitor the health of the trees in the forest.

State the area of artificial intelligence that is being used for this task.   **1**

(*c*)   The forest has a Visitor Centre. Visitors can use a program to identify birds they have spotted in the forest.

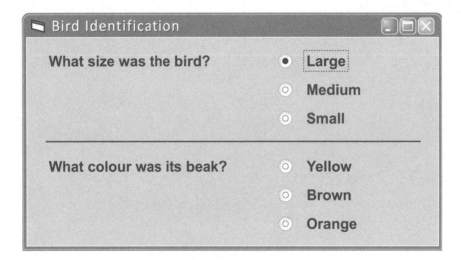

Visitors answer questions about the appearance of the bird. The program identifies the bird, then explains how it reached its conclusion.

(i)   State the type of artificial intelligence program that is being used to identify the birds.   **1**

(ii)   Describe **one** advantage to the visitors of using this type of software, rather than asking a human specialist in wildlife.   **1**

Marks

18. (continued)

(*d*)   The diagram below shows a search tree for a problem.

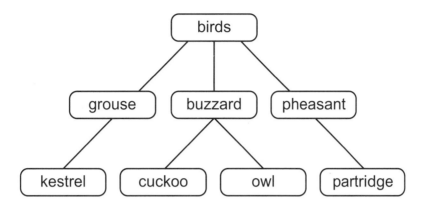

The solution to the problem is **cuckoo**. To reach this solution the nodes were visited in the following order:

birds, grouse, buzzard, pheasant, kestrel, cuckoo

State the type of search that was used here.   1

(5)

[Turn over

Marks

19. The Castello Cruise Company has three cruise ships—Anka, Perla and Marisa. It uses a knowledge base to store facts about the cruises and rules about destinations and special offers. Part of the knowledge base is shown below.

1 departs(anka, southampton).

2 departs(perla, greenock).

3 departs(marisa, greenock).

4 sails_in(anka, july).

5 sails_in(perla, july).

6 sails_in(marisa, august).

7 destination(X, mediterranean):- sails_in(X, july).

8 destination(X, baltic):- sails_in(X, august).

9 special_offer(X):- departs(X, greenock), sails_in(X, august).

(*a*) State the result of the query:

      ? departs(anka, southampton).   **1**

(*b*) State the **first** result of the query:

      ? destination(X, mediterranean).   **1**

(*c*) Using the numbering system to help you, trace how the system evaluates the query:

      ? special_offer(perla).   **3**

(*d*) The Castello Cruise Company updates the knowledge base to include facts about the following extra cruise.

    The Anka departs from Rosyth for the Baltic in August.

    Write the **two** facts that should be added to the knowledge base.   **2**

(*e*) Draw a *semantic net* to represent the facts:

    has(anka, casino).
    has(anka, cinema).
    seats(cinema, 400).   **3**

(10)

[END OF SECTION III—PART A—ARTIFICIAL INTELLIGENCE]

Marks

SECTION III

Part B—Computer Networking

Attempt ALL questions in this section.

20. TastyKakes has created a website to sell its luxury cupcakes.

    (a) Describe **two** economic benefits for the company in having a website. **2**

    (b) The website for TastyKakes has been designed with *hyperlinks*.

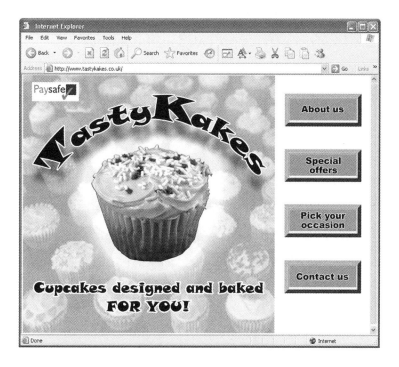

    (i) State **one** function of hyperlinks on the web page. **1**

    (ii) Name the type of software that will allow the user to view this web page. **1**

    (c) The URL for the special offers page is given below.

    http://www.tastykakes.co.uk/specialoffers

    (i) State the domain name of this web page. **1**

    (ii) State the term used for the process of changing a domain name into an Internet Protocol Address (IP Address). **1**

    (d) Customers can order and pay for cupcakes online using a credit card. The website uses *data encryption*.

    (i) Describe what is meant by the term "data encryption". **1**

    (ii) State **one** reason why data encryption is required. **1**

    (e) TastyKakes sends a monthly e-mail to customers on a mailing list.

    State what term is used to describe this method of data transmission. **1**

    (9)

Marks

21. The charity ActiveMind has installed a wireless local area network (WLAN) in its head office.

(a) Describe **one** advantage to the charity of a WLAN compared to a LAN.   1

(b) State **one** item of hardware that is required so that a laptop can be connected to a WLAN.   1

(c) The charity is organising a sponsored fun run to raise funds. The sponsor form is available to download at the address:

ftp://activemind.org

(i) Name the Internet service provided at this address.   1

(ii) Describe **one** problem that can result from downloading files.   1

(iii) Describe **one** other method of transferring a file across the Internet.   1

(d) The charity is worried about the effect of hardware failure on the operation of the network.

(i) State **two** other potential threats to the computer network.   2

(ii) Describe an effective backup strategy that would minimise the effect of a hardware failure to the network.   2

(e) ActiveMind monitors their employees' use of computer technology at work. Describe **two** types of monitoring allowed under the Regulation of Investigatory Powers Act 2000.   2

(11)

Marks

22. Cook-E software allows users to control the operation of their cooker at home from their computer at work.

    (*a*) Cook-E software is an example of *converging technology*.

        Describe what is meant by the term "converging technology".   1

    (*b*) Describe **one** reason why a broadband connection would be recommended for controlling the operation of their cooker.   1

    (*c*) Cook-E software can also be accessed from a mobile phone.

      (i) Name the protocol that allows the software to be accessed from a mobile phone.   1

      (ii) Name the type of software that is needed to access the World Wide Web using a mobile phone.   1

    (*d*) After testing Cook-E software for two months, the user interface is updated.

        State which stage in the software development process is being carried out.   1

                                                    (5)

[END OF SECTION III—PART B—COMPUTER NETWORKING]

Marks

SECTION III

Part C—Multimedia Technology

Attempt ALL questions in this section.

23. Marcus is a final year fashion student who has created a multimedia presentation of his fashion show. He recorded a video of his fashion show and then transferred it to the computer to be edited.

    (a) State **one** item of hardware that is needed to capture video. 1

    (b) State **one** file type that could be used to store the video of the fashion show. 1

    (c) Marcus created a MIDI soundtrack to play over the images of his fashion show.

        (i) State **one** advantage of using a MIDI soundtrack rather than digitised sound. 1

        (ii) State **two** attributes of a MIDI instruction. 2

    (d) The video clip of the fashion show is high quality but the file size is too large. To reduce the size of the video clip, Marcus changes the length of the video clip.

        (i) Describe **two** other ways of reducing the video file size. 2

        (ii) The final size of the file is 4·2 Gigabytes.

            State an appropriate backing storage medium for distributing the presentation to all fashion stores in Britain. 1

            (8)

Marks

24. Brian is using a *WYSIWYG editor* to create a website for a new band.

(a) State **one** other method of creating the website.   **1**

(b) Name **one** device that would allow Brian to capture images of the band for the website.   **1**

(c) Brian records the band's new song "Young Spirit" at their concert. Brian uses audio software to change the *sampling frequency*. He selects the highest frequency for recording the song.

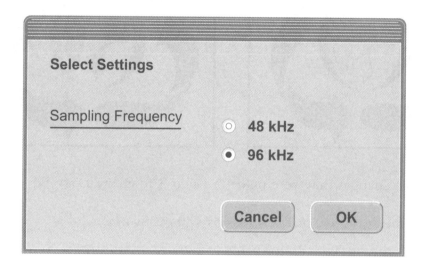

(i) State **one** effect on the size of the sound file of recording the song at the higher setting.   **1**

(ii) State **one** effect on the quality of the sound of recording the song at the higher setting.   **1**

(d) Brian wants to include part of the song "Young Spirit" on the website.

(i) State the feature of the sound editing software that will allow Brian to create a 60 second sample of the song.   **1**

(ii) State **one** other feature of the sound editing software that Brian could use to enhance the sound.   **1**

(e) An interview with the band is available to download from the website as a compressed audio file. The audio file uses *lossy compression*.

(i) Explain what is meant by the term "lossy compression".   **1**

(ii) State a sound file type that uses lossy compression.   **1**

(8)

[Turn over for Question 25 on *Page twenty*

Marks

25. Naila designed a black and white logo for the local recycling campaign using a *bit-mapped graphics package*.

Logo A   **Logo B**

(a) State **two** changes that were made to Logo A to create Logo B.   2

(b) Logo B measures 640 pixels across by 480 pixels down.

Calculate the storage requirements of Logo B in Kilobytes.
Show all working.   2

(c) Naila creates a colour version of Logo B. She then increases the *colour depth* of Logo B.

   (i) State what is meant by the term "colour depth".   1

   (ii) Describe the effect of increasing the colour depth on the size of the file.   1

(d) When the logo was enlarged and then printed, it did not appear as expected.

State **one** reason why bit-mapped graphics lose their quality when enlarged.   1

(e) Naila could save Logo B as either a JPEG file or a GIF file.

Describe **one** difference between JPEG files and GIF files.   1

(f) The logo could have been created using a *vector graphics package*.

State the effect that this would have had on the file size.   1

                                                                                        (9)

[*END OF SECTION III—PART C—MULTIMEDIA TECHNOLOGY*]

[*END OF QUESTION PAPER*]

INTERMEDIATE 2

2011

[BLANK PAGE]

X206/201

NATIONAL
QUALIFICATIONS
2011

FRIDAY, 3 JUNE
9.00 AM – 10.30 AM

COMPUTING
INTERMEDIATE 2

Attempt Section I and Section II and **one** Part of Section III.

Section I – Attempt all questions.

Section II – Attempt all questions.

Section III– This section has three parts:

> Part A – Artificial Intelligence
>
> Part B – Computer Networking
>
> Part C – Multimedia Technology

Choose **one** part and answer **all** of the questions in that part.

Read each question carefully.

Write your answers in the answer book provided. **Do not** write on the question paper.

Write as neatly as possible.

Answer in sentences wherever possible.

Marks

SECTION I

Attempt ALL questions in this section.

1. Arrange the following *memory capacities* into order from the smallest to the biggest.

   terabyte   **kilobyte**   **megabyte**   1

2. State **one** method of spreading a computer virus.   1

3. Name the part of the processor where data is stored temporarily.   1

4. Maria uses both a laptop and a palmtop computer to store data for her business.

   State **one** *input device* that you would find on a laptop but not on a palmtop.   1

5. State **one** *standard file format* that could be used to save a word processed file.   1

6. Convert the binary number 11011 into a decimal number.   1

7. Name **one** *input device* that could be used to capture a graphic.   1

8. A bank's employee is checking that a computer has enough RAM to load a new software package.

   Name the document produced with the software that could help the employee.   1

9. *Macros* can be set up when using applications.

   Describe **one** method of creating and using a macro.   2

10. *Normal* and *extreme* data are used to test a computer program.

    State **one** other type of test data that should be used to test the program.   1

Marks

11. A program has been created to allow student details to be stored.

    (a) State the *variable type* that should be used to store the address of a student.   **1**

    (b) State **one** method a programmer could use to make the program *readable*.   **1**

12. The following is a line of pseudocode used to calculate the volume of a cuboid:

    volume = height multiplied by length squared

    Using an appropriate high level language with which you are familiar, write **program code** for this step of the pseudocode above.   **2**

    (15)

[END OF SECTION I]

[Turn over for Section II

Marks

SECTION II

Attempt ALL questions in this section.

13. Each contestant in the game show "Total Knockout" must compete in five events. A program has been created to calculate the total and average points for each contestant.

The pseudocode for part of this program is shown below.

2.1.	loop 5 times
2.2.	get event points
2.3.	add points to total
2.4.	end loop
2.5.	calculate average points
2.6.	display total and average points

(a) Name **one other** *design notation* that could have been used.   1

(b) Steps 2.1 and 2.4 are the beginning and the end of a *fixed loop*.

Explain why a fixed loop is used here.   1

(c) Using a high level language with which you are familiar, write the line of **program code** for step 2.5 of the algorithm.   2

(d) The names of 50 contestants have to be stored.

State the data structure that should be used to store all the contestants' names.   1

(e) The program design is updated to display an error message if the points entered are not in the range 5 to 25 inclusive. Step 2.2 of the algorithm is refined to include the *conditional statement* shown below.

IF (points<5) AND (points>=25) THEN
display error message
END IF

(i) Identify **two** mistakes made in the above pseudocode.   2

(ii) Name the *standard algorithm* that is used to check that values entered are within a correct range.   1

(iii) The program is to be tested using 8 and 21 as examples of *normal* test data for the points.

State **two** numbers that should be used for *extreme* test data.   2

Marks

13. (continued)

(*f*) A *text editor* is used at the implementation stage.

Describe **one** feature of a text editor.   1

(*g*) Each contestant is given a certificate at the end of the game show.

State **one** reason why a laser printer is used to print a certificate for each of the 50 contestants rather than an inkjet printer.   1

(12)

[Turn over

Marks

14. Antiques can be bought and sold on the BargainSearch website.

(a) Kamila is selling her antique vase. She has taken a black and white photograph of the vase. The photograph measures 2 inches by 3 inches and has a resolution of 800 dpi.

　(i) Calculate the storage requirements of the photograph in Kilobytes.
　　Show all working. 　3

　(ii) Kamila uploaded her photograph to the website. The camera was connected to her computer system through a USB *interface*.

　　State **one** function of an interface. 　1

(b) The reserve price of the vase is £42·50.

　State how a real number such as 42·50 would be represented in the computer. 　1

(c) A computer program is written in a high level programming language to keep track of the bids for each antique.

　(i) Name the *standard algorithm* that is required to find the highest bid. 　1

　(ii) State **one** advantage of writing the program in a high level language rather than in machine code. 　1

　(iii) The *user interface* for the program is planned on paper.

　　State which stage of the software development process is being carried out. 　1

　(iv) The completed program is compiled.

　　Describe how a *compiler* translates a high level language program into machine code. 　1

(d) Name the legislation that BargainSearch must comply with when storing customer information. 　1

(10)

Marks

15. RepairIT uses application software to create an advert.

(*a*) The advert shown above was created using a graphics package.

From this advert, identify **one** object and **one** operation that may have been carried out on that object. 2

(*b*) RepairIT sends the advert to their regular customers by e-mail.

State **one** feature of e-mail that would allow RepairIT to send the advert to all its customers in one operation. 1

(*c*) RepairIT is advertising the Vision 2011 *operating system.*

State **two** functions of an operating system. 2

(*d*) RepairIT is setting up a *LAN* in the resource centre of the local library.

(i) State **one** advantage of using a LAN instead of stand-alone computers. 1

(ii) One computer is to be used as the *file server.*

Describe **one** function of a file server. 1

(*e*) RepairIT offers free *anti-virus software* with every purchase.

Describe **one** purpose of anti-virus software. 1

(8)

[*END OF SECTION II*]

[Turn over

[BLANK PAGE]

SECTION III

Attempt ONE part of Section III

Choose **one** part and answer **all** of the questions in that part.

[Turn over

SECTION III

Marks

Part A—Artificial Intelligence

Attempt ALL questions in this section.

16. Sanjeev is revising for his artificial intelligence assessment using the website PassComputing.

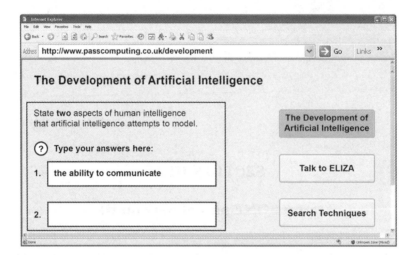

(*a*) Sanjeev selects "The Development of Artificial Intelligence" button. He types "the ability to communicate" as his first answer.

State **one other** aspect of human intelligence that artificial intelligence attempts to model.   1

(*b*) Sanjeev selects the "Talk to ELIZA" button. ELIZA was one of the first examples of a natural language processing application.

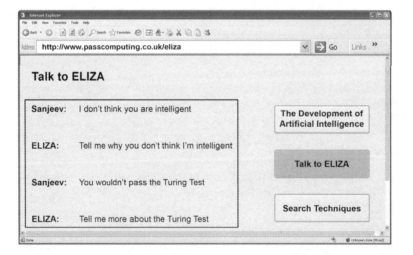

(i) ELIZA would not pass the *Turing Test*.

Describe the Turing Test.   2

(ii) Describe **one** reason why ELIZA shows only limited intelligence.   1

(iii) State **one** recent type of language processing application.   1

(*c*) Sanjeev downloads revision notes.

State **one** suitable backing storage device for storing the downloaded files.   1

Marks

17. Mr MacDonald is testing a new robotic farmer called CropMaster. CropMaster sprays crops, removes weeds and picks fruit.

(a) (i) State **one** application of artificial intelligence that CropMaster could use to identify the weeds. 1

   (ii) Describe **one** problem that could affect the accuracy of CropMaster in correctly identifying the weeds. 1

(b) CropMaster uses an *Artificial Neural System* to help forecast the weather so that the farmer can decide when to harvest his crops.

   (i) What is an Artificial Neural System? 1

   (ii) State **one** disadvantage of using an Artificial Neural System for this purpose. 1

(c) After testing CropMaster for two months, Mr MacDonald is asked to comment on how effective the robotic farmer is at identifying weeds.

   State which stage of the software development process is being carried out. 1

(d) Mr MacDonald also uses an expert system called HealthyHerd to help him diagnose illnesses in his farm animals.

   (i) State **two** advantages to the farmer of using the expert system HealthyHerd rather than consulting a vet. 2

   (ii) State **one** example of a hardware development, other than higher capacity hard drives, that has allowed expert systems to be more effective. 1

   (8)

[Turn over

Marks

18. CoolCamera offers discounted digital cameras and printers. The knowledge base holds facts and rules about cameras on offer.

1	cost(maxpix, 110).	*(camera maxpix costs £110)*
2	cost(megashoot, 220).	
3	cost(powershoot, 105).	
4	cost(photomaster, 225).	
5	oldmodel(fastpics).	*(camera fastpics is an old model)*
6	oldmodel(compactcamera).	
7	megapixels(maxpix, 4).	*(camera maxpix has 4 megapixels)*
8	megapixels(megashoot, 6).	
9	megapixels(powershoot, 12).	
10	megapixels(photomaster, 10).	
11	free_printer(X) if 　　oldmodel(X).	*(camera X gets a free printer if X is an old model)*
12	special_deal(X) if 　　cost(X,Y) and Y>200.	*(camera X is a special deal if X is a camera with cost Y and Y is greater than £200)*

(a) (i) State the result of the following query:

? cost(megashoot, 120).   **1**

(ii) State the result of the following query:

? megapixels(X, 12).   **1**

(b) State the **first** result of the following query:

? free_printer(X).   **1**

(c) Using the numbering system to help you, trace how the system will evaluate the query:

? special_deal(X).

as far as the **first** solution.   **4**

(d) Editing software is free with cameras that have more than 10 megapixels.

Use this information to complete the rule:

free_software(X)   **2**

(e) The knowledge base was written in a declarative language that uses *depth first search*.

Describe what is meant by a depth first search. You may use a diagram to illustrate your answer.   **2**

(11)

[END OF SECTION III—PART A—ARTIFICIAL INTELLIGENCE]

Marks

SECTION III

Part B—Computer Networking

Attempt ALL questions in this section.

19. Eilidh uses a mobile phone, mp3 player and laptop to communicate and play music.

(a) Eilidh speaks to a friend using her mobile phone.

Explain why this is an example of *unicast transmission*.   **1**

(b) Eilidh also uses her mobile phone to access the World Wide Web.

Name the type of software Eilidh is using to access and view web pages on her mobile phone.   **1**

(c) Eilidh can connect her mobile phone, mp3 player and laptop wirelessly so that she can share data.

(i) Name this type of network.   **1**

(ii) Name the hardware that must be installed in each of these devices to allow wireless communication.   **1**

(d) State **one** example of *file transfer* when Eilidh is using her mobile phone, mp3 player or laptop.   **1**

(5)

[Turn over

Marks

20. A website has been created for Lowland High School.

(a) Name the stage of the software development process at which the website is created.   **1**

(b) The school requires an *ISP*.

   (i) What does ISP stand for?   **1**

   (ii) Explain why the school requires an ISP.   **1**

(c) The school's website *URL* is:

     http://www.lowlandhs.sch.uk

What does URL stand for?   **1**

When the website is loaded, the home page is displayed. The home page is shown below.

(d) Name the part of the computer that stores this home page when it is loaded.   **1**

(e) State the method of *navigation* used in this home page.   **1**

(f) The Head Teacher only wants staff to have access to the reports page.

State **one** *software security measure* that could be taken to ensure that only staff can access this web page.   **1**

(g) The school sells calendars, pens and diaries via the website.

Name the type of *e-commerce* service that the school is providing.   **1**

(h) State **one** reason why the school may require *Internet filtering*.   **1**

(9)

Marks

21. UPac is a packaging company which has decided to sell goods online.

(*a*) State **two** *financial* benefits to UPac of selling goods online.   2

(*b*) Name **one** *type of connection* UPac's computers should use to ensure fast Internet access.   1

(*c*) Explain why *encryption* is used when sending confidential files across the Internet.   1

(*d*) Staff are trained on an appropriate code of conduct when using the Internet.

Suggest **two** ways in which the staff could break this code of conduct.   2

(*e*) UPac uses *Domain Name Services* (DNS) to provide *host name resolution* across their network.

State **one** benefit to UPac of using host name resolution.   1

(*f*) UPac has been advised to make a backup of their data.

(i) State **two** reasons why UPac need to backup their data.   2

(ii) UPac uses a tape drive to backup their data.

Describe a suitable backup strategy UPac could use.   2

(11)

[END OF SECTION III—PART B—COMPUTER NETWORKING]

Marks

SECTION III

Part C—Multimedia Technology

Attempt ALL questions in this section.

22.   Murdo has created a *presentation* to demonstrate what it is like to work on a trawler. One of the pages is shown below.

(a)   Murdo asks his friends to check that the video clips are working properly.

   Name the stage of the software development process that is being carried out.   **1**

(b)   Murdo used a *digital camera* to capture the photograph of the boat.

   Name the **type** of storage used to store this photograph within the camera.   **1**

(c)   Image A has been edited to produce Image B.

Image A	Image B

   (i)   State the *image editing* feature that has been used to produce Image B.   **1**

Marks

22. (c) (continued)

Image B has been edited to produce Image C.

Image B   **Image C**

(ii)   State the *image editing* feature that has been used to produce Image C.   1

(iii) State the effect on the file size after Image B is edited to produce Image C.   1

Each video clip in the presentation can play for 30 minutes.

(d) State the hardware device that must be installed within the computer before the video can play.   1

(e) Murdo wants to take his presentation to a college.

(i)   State the most appropriate type of *backing storage media* that he should use.   1

(ii) Murdo copies his presentation onto one of the computers at the college. Unfortunately the file will not run on the college's computer.

State **one** reason why this could have happened.   1

(f) Murdo wants to create a web page using the information in his presentation. He decides to use a *WYSIWYG editor*.

(i)   Name **one** other type of editor Murdo could use.   1

(ii) State **one** benefit to Murdo of using a WYSIWYG editor to create the web page in this case.   1

(10)

[Turn over

Marks

23. An orchestra is recording a new song using digital technology.

    (a) Name **two** hardware devices that the computer must have in order to capture sound.   **2**

    (b) The orchestra play back the recorded song. They notice that the quality of the recording is poor. It is decided to increase the *sampling depth*.

        (i) State **one** implication of increasing the sampling depth.   **1**

        (ii) Suggest **one** other method that could be used to improve the quality when recording sound.   **1**

    (c) The song is edited using *sound editing software*. Name **one** feature of sound editing software that will allow the song to be edited.   **1**

    (d) A musician suggests using a *MIDI keyboard* to create the song.

    State **one** benefit of using a MIDI keyboard.   **1**

    (e) The orchestra use a *digital video camera* to create a video for the song.

        (i) State **one** benefit of using a digital video camera rather than a *webcam* to capture this video.   **1**

        (ii) Name **one** *compressed file format* for storing video.   **1**

                                                                  (8)

Marks

24. A *vector graphics package* has been used to create the following logos for a bicycle company.

Logo A

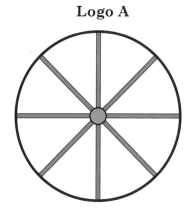

Logo B

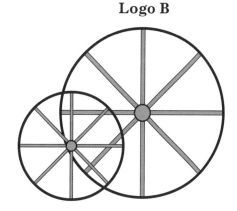

(a) State **one** reason why a *bit-mapped package* would **not** be appropriate for creating these logos.

1

(b) Name **two** features of a vector graphics package that have been used to produce Logo B from Logo A.

2

(c) Name **one** file type that could be used to store vector graphics.

1

(d) Name **one** attribute that is unique to a 3D graphic but not a 2D graphic.

1

(e) Explain why *compression* is often used with *bit-mapped* graphics.

1

(f) State the law that protects the bicycle company's logos from being used by another company without their permission.

1

(7)

[END OF SECTION III—PART C—MULTIMEDIA TECHNOLOGY]

[END OF QUESTION PAPER]

[BLANK PAGE]

[BLANK PAGE]

X206/11/01

| NATIONAL QUALIFICATIONS 2012 | THURSDAY, 31 MAY 1.00 PM – 2.30 PM | COMPUTING INTERMEDIATE 2 |

Attempt Section I and Section II and **one** Part of Section III.

Section I – Attempt all questions.

Section II – Attempt all questions.

Section III– This section has three parts:

        Part A – Artificial Intelligence

        Part B – Computer Networking

        Part C – Multimedia Technology

Choose **one** part and answer **all** of the questions in that part.

Read each question carefully.

Write your answers in the answer book provided. **Do not** write on the question paper.

Write as neatly as possible.

Answer in sentences wherever possible.

SECTION I

Marks

Attempt ALL questions in this section.

1. Name the part of the processor that temporarily stores data and program instructions.   **1**

2. State **one** reason why computer systems use binary numbers rather than decimal numbers.   **1**

3. John's computer is infected by a virus.

   (*a*) Describe **one** way in which a computer virus could be spread.   **1**

   (*b*) State the law that is broken by deliberately spreading a computer virus.   **1**

4. State the type of *main memory* that stores programs and data permanently.   **1**

5. Describe **one** economic factor that has led to the widespread use of computer networks.   **1**

6. A digital camera has a built-in computer system.

   Name this type of computer system.   **1**

7. A scanner is connected to a computer system using an *interface*.

   Explain why an interface is required.   **1**

8. A *macro* is used to carry out a function in an application program.

   Describe **one** method of creating a macro.   **1**

9. A program asks the user to enter an eight character password.

   Name the *standard algorithm* that a program would use to check the number of characters in a password.   **1**

10. A program asks the user to enter an address.

    State the type of variable used to store the name of a city.   **1**

Marks

11. Program code must be *readable*.

Describe **one** way of improving the readability of a program. 1

12. State **one** use of a *text editor* at the implementation stage of the software development process. 1

13. A program written in a *high level language* must be translated.

Describe **one** benefit to the programmer of using an *interpreter* rather than a *compiler* to translate the program code. 1

14. New computer software must be documented.

State the name of the document that explains the features available in the new software. 1

(15)

[END OF SECTION I]

[Turn over for Section II

SECTION II

Marks

Attempt ALL questions in this section.

15. Kirsten wants to buy a new laptop.

    The specifications of two possible laptops are shown below.

Laptop Name	RACER	CAM 12
Processor	2·6 GHz	2·3 GHz
RAM	3 Gb	2 Gb
Magnetic Drive	500 Gb Hard Drive	750 Gb Hard Drive

    (a) The RACER laptop has a 2·6 GHz processor.

    Explain what is meant by 2·6 GHz.   1

    (b) Kirsten buys the RACER laptop as it has more RAM.

    Describe **one** advantage of having more RAM.   1

    (c) Kirsten's old laptop has a *floppy disk drive*.

    State **one** reason why modern computers do **not** have floppy disk drives. 1

    (d) Kirsten buys an *optical drive* for the laptop.

    State a suitable optical disk that she could use with this drive to save and delete data.   1

    (e) Kirsten buys a printer to attach to her new laptop. She decides to buy a *laser printer* rather than an *inkjet printer*.

    State **one** reason why she has chosen the laser printer.   1

    (f) The laptop uses a *character set*.

    Explain what is meant by a character set.   1

    (g) The laptop is installed with an *operating system*.

    State **one** function of an operating system.   1

15. (continued)   *Marks*

    (*h*) Kirsten uses her laptop to create a letter to send to her insurance company. She saves the letter using a *standard file format*.

        (i) State the standard file format that keeps the **formatting** of the letter.   **1**

       (ii) The finished letter requires **32 Kb** of storage.

           Convert this file size into **bytes**.   **1**

      (iii) A laptop is a type of portable computer system.

           Name **one** other type of portable computer.   **1**

                                     (10)

[Turn over

Marks

16. An international language school uses a *mainframe computer system* to process candidates' exam results from 50 different countries. A program is being created to analyse these results.

    (a) State **two** reasons why the language school uses a mainframe computer system to run the program.   2

    (b) State the *standard algorithm* the program should use to find the country that has the lowest number of candidates sitting exams.   1

    (c) The number of candidates for **each** of the 50 countries needs to be stored.

    State the data structure required.   1

    (d) One of the program's tasks is to calculate the total number of candidates for **all** 50 countries. Part of the design is shown below.

1.   Set overall total to zero
2.
3.   get country total
4.   add country total to overall total
5.   end loop
6.   display overall total

    Complete step 2 of the design.   1

16. (continued)   *Marks*

(e) The candidate's date of birth is printed on their exam certificate. The program checks that the date of birth is valid.

Date of birth: **day/month/year**

Example: **10/06/1994**

Part of the design used to validate the **month** input is shown below.

2.1	get month
2.2	if _____ then
2.3	display error message
2.4	end if

(i) Complete step 2.2 of the design above.   2

(ii) This part of the design needs to be repeated until correct.

State the **type** of loop required.   1

(f) The following test data is used to check the **month** of the candidate's date of birth.

Normal	06
Extreme	
Exceptional	13

(i) What could be the missing input for extreme data?   1

(ii) Explain the importance of thoroughly testing a program.   1

                                                                        (10)

[Turn over

Marks

17. Dave owns a company called Classic Cars. He decides to employ a software developer to create a program to help him process data. The following design has been created.

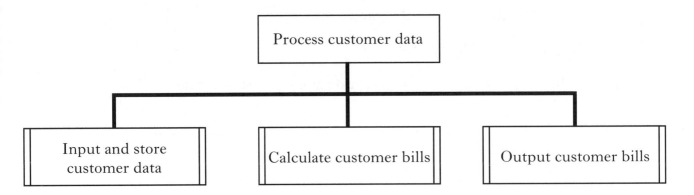

(a) State the *graphical design notation* used above.   1

(b) State the stage of the software development process that involves creating the program code.   1

(c) The software developer decides to use a *high level language* to create the program.

State **two** reasons why a high level language is used rather than *machine code*.   2

(d) The software developer uses *pre-defined functions* within the program.

Explain **one** benefit to the software developer of using pre-defined functions.   1

(e) The software developer creates *readable* program code.

State **one** reason why readable code helps future maintenance.   1

(f) The program is now complete and fully tested.

State **one** reason why it is important to produce a *technical guide*.   1

17. (continued)   *Marks*

(g) Dave decides to advertise his company using a website.

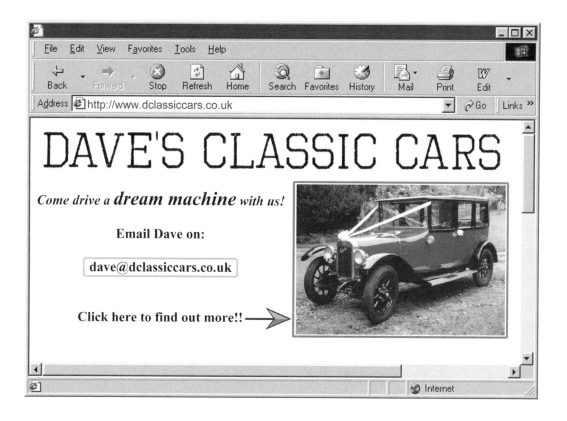

(i) When a user clicks on the graphic of the car, another page on Dave's website is shown.

Name this navigation feature.   1

(ii) Dave adds a video clip to the website.

State why high *bandwidth* is recommended for viewing this video clip.   1

(iii) Apart from cost, state **one** advantage to Dave of using *e-mail* to communicate with customers.   1

(10)

[END OF SECTION II]

[Turn over

[BLANK PAGE]

SECTION III

Attempt ONE part of Section III

Choose **one** part and answer **all** of the questions in that part.

[Turn over

SECTION III

Marks

Part A—Artificial Intelligence

Attempt ALL questions in this section.

18. DomesticDiva is an intelligent robot that has been programmed to clean floors.

    (a) DomesticDiva has been fitted with sensors so that it can move about the house without bumping into the furniture.

    Name **two** sensors that would help the robot detect the furniture.   **2**

    (b) DomesticDiva responds to spoken commands such as START, STOP and CLEAN.

        (i) State the area of artificial intelligence that is being used by the robot to understand spoken commands.   **1**

        (ii) State **two** factors that may make communication with the robot difficult.   **2**

    (c) DomesticDiva uses artificial intelligence to understand the layout of the house from photographs.

    State the area of artificial intelligence that is being used for this task.   **1**

    (d) State **one** development in hardware, other than faster processors, that has made progress in the field of artificial intelligence research possible.   **1**

    (7)

Marks

19. The TV favourite Lions' Den has launched a website to help people get cash investment for their business ideas.

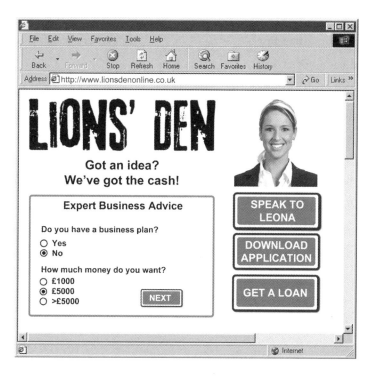

(*a*) An *expert system* can be accessed from the website.

   (i) Explain what is meant by an expert system.   **1**

   (ii) State **two** advantages of using the expert system rather than consulting a human expert.   **2**

(*b*) A natural language program called "Leona" is used to answer simple questions. Leona simulates conversation with a human.

   Name this type of natural language processing application.   **1**

(*c*) A user downloads an application form to a palmtop computer system.

   State **one** input device that could be used to complete the application form.   **1**

(*d*) Business users can apply online for loans. An *artificial neural system* is used to assess the risk of giving loans.

   (i) Explain what is meant by an artificial neural system.   **1**

   (ii) Describe **one disadvantage** of using an artificial neural system for this task.   **1**

                            (7)

[Turn over

Marks

20. The Royal Theatre in Newtown is organising a weekend of special events. It uses a knowledge base to store facts and rules about events and tickets. Part of the knowledge base is shown below.

1	showing_on(opera,saturday).	*(Opera is showing on Saturday)*
2	showing_on(dance,saturday).	
3	showing_on(storytelling,sunday).	
4	costs(dance,3).	*(Dance costs £3)*
5	costs(opera,7).	
6	costs(storytelling,4).	
7	suitable_for(dance,adults).	*(Dance is suitable for adults)*
8	suitable_for(opera,adults).	
9	suitable_for(storytelling,children).	
10	family_show(X) if suitable_for(X,children).	*(X is a family show if X is suitable for children)*
11	get_free_ticket(X) if costs(X,Y) and Y>5.	*(Get a free ticket for X if X costs Y and Y is greater than £5)*

(*a*) (i) State the result of the following query:

    ? showing_on(dance,sunday).   **1**

(ii) State the result of the following query:

    ? family_show(X).   **1**

(*b*) Using the numbering system to help you, *trace* how the system will evaluate the query:

    ? get_free_ticket(X).   **4**

(*c*) One way of representing information before creating a knowledge base is by using a *semantic net*.

(i) Draw a semantic net to represent the facts:

    likes(jess, comedy).
    likes(jess, dance).
    features(dance, ballet).   **3**

(ii) Name the stage of the software development process at which a semantic net will be drawn.   **1**

20. (continued)   *Marks*

(*d*) The following search tree illustrates a search through a knowledge base.

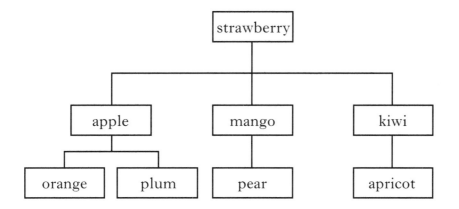

The solution to the problem is pear.
The nodes are visited in the following order:

    strawberry   apple   mango   kiwi   orange   plum   pear

State the type of search that has been used here.   **1**

                                                                                                     (11)

[END OF SECTION III—PART A—ARTIFICIAL INTELLIGENCE]

[Turn over

SECTION III   *Marks*

Part B—Computer Networking

Attempt ALL questions in this section.

21. The BST bank uses the Internet to advertise, sell financial services and communicate with customers. By using the Internet the bank has saved money on staffing and other costs.

   (a) Apart from costs, state **two** other advantages to the **bank** of using the Internet for these purposes.   2

   (b) Bank customers can download an application program from the bank's website to view balances on their mobile phone.

   State the Internet service that is used to download the application program.   1

   (c) Mobile phones use *WAP* technology and *microbrowsers*.

      (i) What is a microbrowser?   1

     (ii) State **one** reason why mobile phones use microbrowsers.   1

   (d) The bank upgrades the website to allow customers to transfer money between accounts.

   Name the stage of the software development process being carried out.   1

   (e) The bank's website has a help page. Customers use the following URL to access this help page:

                    http://www.bstbank.co.uk/help

      (i) Name the *protocol* used by this URL.   1

     (ii) Describe how the *Domain Name Service* (*DNS*) would find this URL on the Internet.   2

    (iii) State **one** limitation of using *domain names* across the Internet.   1

                                          (10)

Marks

22. The McTavish family connects their three computer systems and a printer wirelessly within their home.

(*a*) Name this type of network. 　　　　1

(*b*) State **one** additional hardware requirement for setting up this network. 　　　　1

(*c*) State **one** advantage of using a wireless connection compared to a cabled connection. 　　　　1

(*d*) They now decide to connect their three computers to the Internet.

State **one** reason why they need an ISP. 　　　　1

(*e*) The family access the Internet to stream video.

State the type of Internet connection required for this task. 　　　　1

(*f*) Describe **one** *software security* feature the parents could use to prevent the children accessing inappropriate content on the Internet. 　　　　1

(*g*) Explain what the family should do to avoid accidentally downloading computer *viruses* from the Internet. 　　　　1

(7)

[Turn over

Marks

23. A data transmission company installs and sells Internet connections.

    (*a*) State **two** reasons why there is no longer a demand for the company to supply and install *dial up modems*.   **2**

    (*b*) The police are interested in purchasing a fast, secure and dedicated connection to the Internet.

        (i) State the type of connection the company should recommend to the police.   **1**

        (ii) State **two types** of network threats that could lead to failure of the police computer network.   **2**

    (*c*) The company also sells *encryption* software.

    Explain what happens when data is encrypted.   **1**

    (*d*) The company is investing in televisions that allow multi-user gaming across the Internet.

        (i) State **one** other task this type of television could perform to suggest it is an appliance that uses *converging technologies*.   **1**

        (ii) State **one** other example of an appliance that uses converging technologies in the home.   **1**

(8)

[END OF SECTION III—PART B—COMPUTER NETWORKING]

SECTION III   *Marks*

Part C—Multimedia Technology

Attempt ALL questions in this section.

24. Nihal is creating a website for a local cycling shop to advertise mountain bikes for sale and cycling skills courses.

 (*a*) Nihal discusses the requirements of the website with the manager of the cycling shop.

 Name the stage of the software development process that Nihal is carrying out.   **1**

 (*b*) Nihal takes photographs for the website using his digital camera.

 (i) The digital camera makes use of a CCD.

 Describe the function of a CCD in a digital camera.   **1**

 (ii) Each photograph has a file size of 2·4 Mb. The digital camera memory card has a capacity of 2 Gb.

 Calculate how many images can be stored on the memory card.

 Show all working.   **2**

 (iii) Nihal edits Photograph A to produce Photograph B as shown below.

 State which feature of the image editing software Nihal has used.   **1**

Photograph A   Photograph B

 (iv) Nihal's photographs are saved as JPEG files. JPEG files use *lossy compression*.

 Explain what is meant by lossy compression.   **1**

 (*c*) Nihal is advised to use a *WYSIWYG editor* to create the website.

 (i) Describe how a WYSIWYG editor would be used to create his website.   **1**

 (ii) Name **one** other method that could be used to create the website.   **1**

24. (continued)   *Marks*

(*d*) Nihal records a video on bike maintenance for the website. He saves the video file and then uploads it to the website for viewing.

(i) State the **most appropriate** item of hardware that is used to capture video.   1

(ii) State **one** file type that could be used to store the video.   1

(iii) The video is very jerky when played.

Explain how Nihal could alter the settings in the video recording software to ensure that the video is not jerky.   1

                                                                              (11)

25. Homes4U has a multimedia DVD to advertise its luxurious flats.

(*a*) The background music for the DVD was recorded using a microphone.

The recording software allows the settings to be altered.

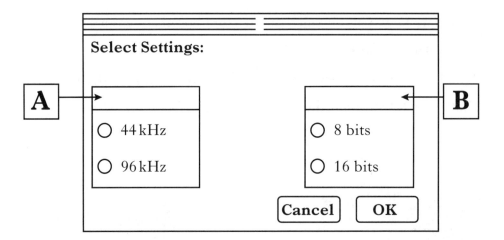

(i) State the name of the setting for A.   1

(ii) State the name of the setting for B.   1

(iii) State which *standard file format* for digitised sound would give the best quality sound with the smallest file size.   1

(iv) Instead of recording sound with a microphone, the sound could have been synthesised.

(A) Describe **one** way of creating sound in this way.   1

(B) State the file format that would be used to store the information from the synthesised music.   1

25. (continued)   *Marks*

    (*b*) The DVD includes a *virtual reality* guide to the luxurious flats.

        (i) Explain the benefit of using virtual reality rather than a slideshow of images to advertise the flats.   **1**

      (ii) State **one** specialised input device that could be used with this virtual reality application.   **1**

    (*c*) Multimedia files can be run as executable files.

        State **one** other way that you could run multimedia files on a computer system.   **1**

                                                      (8)

[Turn over

Marks

26. A *vector graphics package* was used to create a company logo for a local optician.

(a) Name **two** attributes of the circle objects used in the logo.   2

(b) Name **one** file type used to store graphics in vector format.   1

(c) Describe **two** advantages of a vector graphic over a bit-mapped graphic.   2

(d) The logo is displayed on a large monitor in the optician's window.
    State the item of hardware that is required to display graphics on the monitor.   1

                                                                                      (6)

[END OF SECTION III—PART C—MULTIMEDIA TECHNOLOGY]

[END OF QUESTION PAPER]

[BLANK PAGE]

[BLANK PAGE]

SQA INTERMEDIATE 2
COMPUTING 2008–2012

INTERMEDIATE 2 COMPUTING 2008

SECTION I

1. *Any two from:*
   - Fewer arithmetic rules
   - 0 and 1 easily represent on and off
   - signal degradation has no effect

2. *Any one from:*
   - Shares resources
   - Shares files
   - Mail server
   - Web server
   - Print server

3. *Any one from:*
   - Compensates for different speeds
   - Converts data
   - Temporarily stores data

4. *Any one from:*
   - To display an error message
   - To warn out of paper, ink low
   - Status signals
   - Preview tasks

5. Pre-prepared list of email addresses lets you contact many people without typing in all the addresses.

6. • Decrease resolution
   • Reduce colour depth
   • Use compression

7. X = Analysis, Y = Implementation

8. (a) Readability
   (b) Record/use a macro

9. Array

10. (a) Discount given
    (b) No discount

11. *Any one from:*
    Washing machine; fridge; microwave oven; CD player

SECTION II

12. (a) Processor
    (b) Backing store
    (c) (i) 2·83 GHz
        (ii) *Any two from:*
            - Hard disk has larger capacity, stores more
            - Hard disk is magnetic storage, CD-R is optical
            - Speed of data transfer is faster on hard disk
            - CDs are portable
            - Hard disk is re-writeable
        (iii) Laptop guide is a hyperlink (hotspot)
        (iv) *Any one from:*
            Webcam; microphone; sound card; graphics card; digital camcorder; smart phone
    (d) Kilobytes = terabytes * 2^30
    (e) It is in machine code - 0 and 1

13. (a) • Loop from 1 to 5
        • Do 5 times
    (b) String
    (c) *Any one from:*
        Structure diagram; flow chart; data flow diagram
    (d) Maintenance
    (e) (i) Input validation
        (ii) Price > 1 and price < 4
        (iii) *Any one from:*
            • Exceptional testing
            • Outside range
            • Testing string
    (f) Object records; Operation SORT

14. (a) Documentation
    (b) Standard format that can be opened on most computers.
    (c) Wide Area Network.
    (d) Linear search
    (e) 20 × 64 **or** 1280 bits
        160 bytes **or** 160
    (f) (i) *Any one from:*
            Floppy disk; USB flash drive; website; infected CD; email attachment.
        (ii) To control the running of a computer system.
    (g) Copyright, Design and Patents Act

SECTION III

Part A – Artificial Intelligence

15. (a) *Any one from:*
        - Retain knowledge
        - Solve problems
        - Recognise objects
    (b) (i) Only repeats keywords, has no understanding
        (ii) Turing test
        (iii) *Any one from:*
            • Larger hard drive capacity
            • Larger memory (RAM)
            • Faster processor
        (iv) *Any one from:*
            Background noise; accent; sore throat; not speaking clearly.
    (c) (i) *Any one from:*
            Infra red sensors; touch sensor; vision sensor
        (ii) Navigate round the object

16. (a) A program that can give advice like a human expert
    (b) *Any one from:*
        • Expertise always available
        • Combines expertise of several experts
        • Less chance of error
    (c) • Camera photographs apple
        • Image compared to database
    (d) (i) Electronic model of the human brain
        (ii) *Any one from:*
            • It may not contain the most up to date data
            • It may not be able to take special circumstances into account
    (e) Enter Farmers' Market Scotland
        Click GoFind or press enter

17. (*a*) Design

(*b*)

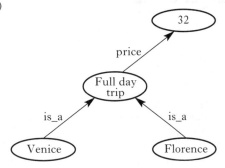

18. (*a*) Yes

(*b*) X = inverness

(*c*) high_risk(oban) matches at 6, X = Oban
Subgoal uv_index(oban, Y)
Matches at 5
Y = 5
Subgoal Y > 4
Succeeds
Yes

(*d*) low_risk(X) if uv_index(X,Y) and
Y < 3

Part B – Computer Networking

19. (*a*) (i) Broadcast

(ii) *Any one from:*
- Receiver/Transmitter
- Wireless router

(iii) *Any one from:*
- Passwords
- Firewall
- WEP/encryption

(*b*) (i) If using dial-up then she will not be charged while she is typing the email if off-line.

(ii) *Any one from:*
- Dial-up
- Wireless

(*c*) (i) *Any one from:*
- Not to send large unnecessary attachments
- Use email for professional purposes only

(ii) *Any one from:*
- Non profit organisation
- Charity

(iii) Attachment

20. (*a*) (i)
- Enter Tennis clubs and Livingston in the search box
- Press return or click Search

(ii) The filtering software would not allow the search

(iii) Internet Service Provider

(*b*) (i) To code a document so that it cannot be read by anyone who is not supposed to.

(ii) Regulation of Investigatory Powers Act

(iii) *Any one from:*
- Increased sales due to worldwide customer base
- Investment needed for webserver/Web page creation
- Savings on printing manuals and packaging

(*c*) (i) *Any one from:*
- Convert the domain name to an IP address
- Using DNS software to find the IP address

(ii) *Any one from:*
- Encrypt/downloads/manual
- Encrypt/downloads/manual.dok

(iii) Describe the basic functions of the program

(*d*) • Backup regularly
  • Store in a safe place in a different location from the original copy.

21. (*a*) • WPAN
  • PAN

(*b*) • Interface
  • ADC

(*c*) Monitor (or palmtop) could use built-in telecommunications to send message to hospital/doctor/ambulance alerting them of situation.

(*d*) Data transmission failure

Part C – Multimedia Technology

22. (*a*) Convert the light into an electrical signal

(*b*) (i) Design

(ii) • Bits to bytes (/8) = 3670016
  • Bytes to kilobytes (/1024) = 3584
  • Kilobytes to Megabytes (/1024) = 3·5

(*c*) (i) Description of using a toolbar or dragging and dropping pictures and text frames to create the Web page.

(ii) *Any one from:*
- Code for Web page would be typed.
- HTML would be created

(*d*) Transparency

(*e*) *Any one from:*
- Reduce the resolution
- Reduce the colour depth
- Increase degree of compression

23. (*a*) *Any one from:*
- Microphone
- Graphics card
- Sound card

(*b*) (i) *Any one from:*
- Synthesised sound would sound unnatural
- Voice cannot be stored as part of a MIDI file

(ii) *Any one from:*
- Increasing the sampling rate increases the sound quality
- Decreasing the sampling rate decreases the sound quality

(*c*) (i) *Any one from:*
- Sounds not heard by human ear are not encoded
- Sounds drowned out by others are not encoded
- Some sounds are recorded in mono
- Huffman encoding used

(ii) *Any one from:*
- RAW
- AIFF
- CD-DA (Compact Disc Digital Audio)
- WAV
- MIDI

(*d*) (i) *Any one from:*
- The number of pixels in a fixed area
- The number of pixels on the screen

(ii) *Any two from:*
- Increase the frame rate
- Increase the colour depth
- Reduce the degree of compression

(*e*) (i) *Any one from:*
- Play a MIDI instrument connected to the computer
- Use MIDI software to play the notes

(ii) Sound card

(*f*) SmartPhone

24. (*a*) *Any two from:*
- If it scales without loss of quality (resolution) then vector.
- Each object is editable then vector
- Look for a vector file extension
- Each pixel can be edited
- If scaled larger then picture will pixelate
- Two dimensional array of pixels (no layers)
- Look for a bitmap file extension

(*b*) Scalable Vector Graphics

(*c*) Stores the attributes of the object

(*d*) Object - eg ellipse, rectangle
Operation: eg filled with colour

INTERMEDIATE 2 COMPUTING 2009

SECTION I

1. *Any one from:*
- Share files
- Share hardware/peripherals eg printers
- Can access files on any computer
- Security of files
- Communication

2. • Backing storage stores data permanently
- RAM is not permanent
(Both required)

3. ALU

4. Operating system

5. CD-R, DVD-R, DVD+R, CD recordable, DVD recordable, Blu-ray-R

6. Touchscreeen, microphone, reduced keyboard

7. (*a*) 1101

(*b*) A non-printing character that causes an effect

8. *Any one from:*
- Have a clear understanding of exactly what the program is required to do.
- Produce a program specification.

9. *Any one from:*
- Easier to understand
- Easier to edit
- Portability

10. Implementation

11. Speed > 30
And
Speed < 35
(2 marks for all correct; 1 mark for one error)

12. Find maximum

13. Conditional loop

SECTION II

14. (*a*) (i) Pseudocode

(ii) • Structure diagram with description or diagram
• Flow chart with description or diagram

(*b*) The code within the loop must be repeated seven times, once for each day of the week

(*c*) (i) *Any one from:*
- To allow the user to enter source code
- To allow the user to edit source code

(ii) RAM

(*d*) *Any two from:*
- Meaningful variable names
- Meaningful procedure names
- Internal commentary
- Indentation
- Use of white space
- Modularity

(*e*) • Mantissa
• Exponent

15. (a) *Any one from:*
- Object – heading text; operation – font, size of text changed
- Object – image of house/for sale sign; operation – copied, pasted, scaled, rotated, flipped

(b) $3 \times 4 \times 600 \times 600$
= 4,320,000 bits/8
= 540,000 bytes/1024
= 527·3 kilobytes

(c) *Any one from:*
- Compensates for differences in speed/code/format/voltage between the CPU and the peripheral
- Convert from analogue to digital

(d) *Any one from:*
- Faster output of multiple copies
- Cheaper running costs

(e) (i) • Browser
- Communications software

(ii) • Firewall
- Anti-virus software
- Anti-spyware software

(f) Data Protection Act

16. (a) *Any one from:*
- Real
- Integer
- Numeric

(b) (i) Input Validation

(ii) *Any two from:*
- Non numeric eg forty five
- Number out of range eg 200, 80
- Negative number eg -25

(c) *Any one of:*
- Interpreter reports mistakes as they are made
- Faster development time

(d) Technical Guide

(e) (i) Evaluation

(ii) The program meets the specification

(f) (i) *Any one from:*
- Spread via floppy disk
- Homemade CDs
- Websites
- E-mail
- E-mail attachments
- Macros

(ii) *Any one from:*
- Displaying unwanted messages
- Unusual visual or sound effects
- Computers rebooting unexpectedly
- Unwanted generation of emails

SECTION III

Part A – ARTIFICIAL INTELLIGENCE

17. (a) (i) *Any one from:*
- Program following a set of simple rules
- Restricted environment
- Defined set of rules

(ii) Turing test
User communicates with an unseen respondent; if he cannot tell if it is a computer or a person then it is said to be intelligent

(b) (i) ELIZA responds to user's statements by asking questions based on key words from the user's input

(ii) Chatterbot

(c) *Any one from:*
- Used to read postcodes
- Handwriting recognition

(d) (i) *Any one from:*
- Robot uses sensor to detect a physical quantity eg bump, weight
- Robot can find their way from one terminal to another by following wires buried in factory floor (magnetic guidance system)
- Robot follows painted line on ground (light guidance system)
- Rotating laser attached to robot and reflective light hits targets to calculate its position

(ii) *Any one from:*
- Robot doesn't need humans to make decisions
- Robot is able to adapt to new situations
- Learn from mistakes
- No damage or accidents

(e) *Any one from:*
- Faster processors
- Increased RAM
- Increased capacity of hard drives
- Improved sensors
- Improved portable power supplies

18. (a) *Any two from:*
- Many experts' knowledge is available
- Advice is consistent
- Advice is available to many different users at the same time
- May get advice quicker than visiting doctor
- Allow people who are reluctant to discuss complaint to talk to computer program rather than a person
- Don't have to travel to surgery

(b) *Any one from:*
- Moral/ethical implications – who is responsible when advice given is incorrect?
- Doctors fear that they might lose their jobs

(c) (i) Train software to recognise voice

(ii) *Any one from:*
- Background noise
- Sore throat/cold
- Stutter

(iii) *Any one from:*
- Handwriting recognition
- OCR

19. (a) (i) No or false

(ii) X=dominik

(b) Match at line 11
Subgoal 1 fitness(X excellent)
Match at line 1 X = jessica
Subgoal 2 owns(jessica bike) no match subgoal fails
Backtrack, subgoal 1 match at line 2 X = shabir
Subgoal 2 owns(shabir bike) match at line 6

20. (a) Venezuela, Peru, Paraguay, Brazil, Argentina, Chile

(b) (i) Design

(ii)

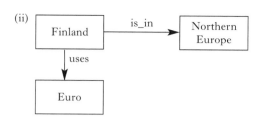

Part B – COMPUTER NETWORKING

21. (a) Hyperlinks **or** Hotspots

   (b) (i) Internet Service Provider

     (ii) File transfer

     (iii) unicast

   (c) (i) isp4scots.co.uk

     (ii) It searches for the URL in its database
and identifies the server where it is stored
or
matches domain name
with an IP address

   (d) More visitors to his site

22. (a) *Any one from:*
- Paying for the website to be designed and created
- Maintenance
- Cost of Internet access

   (b) Microbrowser

   (c) *Any one from:*
- Police investigating a crime
- National security

   (d) (i) Computer Misuse Act

     (ii) *Any two from:*
- Save a copy on second backing storage
- Regularly back up
- Keep backup in safe place away from the original

   (e) (i) *Any two from:*
- Can still receive phone calls
- Not paying for length of time connected to Internet
- Faster transfer of data
- More stable/reliable

     (ii) recruitment

   (f) (i) Wireless personal area network

     (ii) Filtering or explanation of filtering.

23. (a) *Any one from:*
- Can shop 24/7
- Can easily compare prices
- Can do it in comfort of own home

   (b) (i) • Liquid crystal display

     (ii) • Enter model
- Enter code
- Click on Go
(All 3 parts, 2 marks; any 2 parts, 1 mark)

   (c) (i) Embedded

     (ii) *Any one from:*
- Washing machine could have contacted engineer and reported fault
- Software could have been downloaded remotely

Part C – MULTIMEDIA TECHNOLOGY

24. (a) *Any one from:*
- Webcam
- Digital video Camera

   (b) (i) *Any one from:*
- Charge Coupled Device or CCD
- ADC

     (ii) **A)** • The number of bits per pixel
- The number of colours that are possible

       B) • The number of pixels in a fixed area/image
- Dots per Inch (DPI)

     (iii) crop

     (iv) larger file size

   (c) (i) Volume/amplitude

     (ii) Reverse

     (iii) Sound card

   (d) (i) They can navigate the building in 3D

     (ii) VRML/WRL

     (iii) *Any one from:*
- File player
- Browser
- Media player

25. (a) *Any one from:*
- Change resolution
- Crop

   (b) (i) See whole clip/film

     (ii) Video will be jerky

   (c) (i) lossy

     (ii) • Faster download times
- Limited storage capacity on mp3 player

   (d) *Any one from:*
- MIDI keyboard
- Synthesiser

   (e) Maintenance

26. (a) Texture

   (b) (i) • Position
- Colour fill

     (ii) Enlarge the image – not resolution independent

     (iii) transparency

INTERMEDIATE 2 COMPUTING 2010

SECTION I

1. *Any one from:*
- ASCII
- UNICODE

2. Mainframe computer system

3. Arithmetic and Logic Unit (ALU)

4. *Any one from:*
- RTF (Rich Text Format)
- ASCII

5. (a) *Any one from:*
   LAN
   Client server network

   (b) *Any one from:*
   - Faster transmission speed than copper cable
   - More secure data transmission than copper cable
   - No/reduced interface

6. *Any one from:*
- Compensates for differences in
  - Speed
  - Code
  - Format
  - Voltage
- Convert from analogue to digital

7. *Any one from:*
- The interpreter works by translating and then executing each line of the program in turn whereas the compiler translates the program code in one operation
- The compiler saves a machine code file so the program only needs to be translated once whereas the interpreter must translate the program every time it is run

8. Find maximum

9. (a) *Any one from:*
   - Built-in calculation
   - A calculation the software already knows how to carry out

   (b) *Any valid pre-defined function e.g.:*
   RND
   ROUND

10. *Any one from:*
- The program does what it was intended to do
- The program meets the specification
- The program is correct

11. *Any one from:*
- Pseudocode with description
- Flow chart with description
- Semantic Net

12. *Any one from:*
- String variable
- String
- Text/alphanumeric

SECTION II

13. (a) 3·8 GHz (must have GHz)

   (b) (i) 1 Gb or 1024 Mb (must have units)
       (ii) *Any one from:*
       - File management
       - Memory management
       - Input output
       - Error reporting

(iii) Computer Misuse Act

(c) So he can connect more peripherals at the one time

(d) *Any one from:*
- Save video data
- To back up large quantities of data

(e) *Any one from:*
- Magnetic tape drive
- Zip drive

(f) (i) • A = Normal
        • B = 60 or 15 (only 1 required)
        • C = No delivery
    (ii) Distance>=15   **or**   Distance>=15
         AND   AND
         Distance<=60   <=60

14. (a) Graphic of shoe – scaled, rotated
   Text – font, size, bold

   (b) (i) Embedded
       (ii) *Any one from:*
       - Speaker
       - LCD
       - Light
       - Buzzer

   (c) (i) *Any one from:*
       - Numeric
       - Single
       - Real
       (ii) • BMI = weight/height^2
            or
            • BMI = weight/(height*height)
       (iii) *Any one from:*
       - Comment lines
       - Meaningful variable names
       - Good use of white space
       - Indentation
       - Modular
       (iv) If code cannot be understood at a later date changing it will be difficult.

   (d) (i) Using a mailing list
       (ii) *Any one from:*
       - Hyperlink
       - Link
       - Hotspot
       (iii) Data Protection Act

15. (a) *Any two from:*
   - Labels in B more detailed
   - Labels not as detailed in A
   - Less typing in B, can select in B
   - B has help button

   (b) (i) To make sure only suitable data is entered
       (ii) User can only select 50, 100, 200 so cannot enter invalid amount.

   (c) Array

SECTION III

Part A – ARTIFICIAL INTELLIGENCE

16. (a) (i) An electronic model of the brain
        (ii) It will predict if the shares will increase in value
        (iii) *Any one from:*
        - Reading post codes
        - Debt risk assessment
        - Pattern recognition

(b) (i) *Any one from:*
- Ability to communicate
- Retain knowledge
- Solve problems

(ii) Improve through learning from mistakes

(iii) Wide area network

17. (a) *Any one from:*
- Punctuation
- E-mail related – send, reply, forward, attach

(b) Touch sensitive screen

(c) *Any one from:*
- Eliza
- Parry
- SHRDLU

(d) It could speak and tell her what is in her e-mails or diary for the day

18. (a) *Any one from:*
- Can navigate round obstacles
- Can adapt to different sizes of tree

(b) Vision system

(c) (i) Expert system

(ii) *Any one from:*
- Available all the time
- Combines knowledge of several experts

(d) Breadth first

19. (a) Yes
or
True

(b) anka

(c) Matches at 9 X=perla
Subgoal 1
departs(perla, greenock)
Matches at 2
Succeeds
Subgoal 2
Sails_in(perla, august)
Fails
No

(d) departs(anka, rosyth).
sails_in(anka, august).

(e)

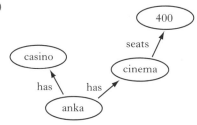

Part B – COMPUTER NETWORKING

20. (a) *Any one from:*
- Increased marketing opportunities
- Increased on-line sales
- Larger customer base
- No shop costs

(b) (i) *Any one from:*
- Improves navigation through the website
- Can move to another page in the website by clicking on a hyperlink
- Idea of clicking to move directly to another part of the website

(ii) Web browser

(c) (i) www.tastykakes.co.uk

(ii) Domain name resolution

(d) (i) Data is encoded

(ii) To provide a secure electronic transaction for customers.

(e) Multicast

21. (a) *Any one from:*
- Computers can be placed anywhere – flexible
- Cheaper to install/set-up
- No trailing cables (Health & Safety)

(b) *Any one from:*
- Wireless network interface card
- Wireless NIC
- Wireless router

(c) (i) File transfer

(ii) Common route for virus attack

(iii) Attaching a file to an e-mail

(d) (i) *Any two from:*
- Software failure eg failure of network operating system, fault with browser
- Data transmission failure eg damaged cables
- Physical disaster eg fire, flood, cuts in electricity supply

(ii) *Any two from:*
- Save a copy of data on a second backing storage medium
- Store backup copies away from the original data in a safe location
- Make regular backup copies of data

(e) • Employers can monitor e-mail traffic
- Employers can track which websites staff visit during work time

22. (a) Home applications that can communicate with other devices and the Internet.

(b) *Any one from:*
- The connection is "always on"
- Faster connection

(c) (i) *Any one from:*
- WAP
- Wireless Application Protocol

(ii) Microbrowser

(d) Maintenance

Part C – MULTIMEDIA TECHNOLOGY

23. (a) Digital video camera

(b) *Any one from:*
- AVI
- MPEG
- MOV

(c) (i) *Any one from:*
- Smaller file size
- Instrument can be changed

(ii) *Any two from:*
- Type of instrument
- Pitch of note
- Volume of note
- Duration of note
- Tempo

(d) (i) *Any two from:*
- Reduce frame rate/frames per second
- Reduce colour depth
- Reduce the resolution of the image

(ii) DVD

24. (a) *Any one from:*
    • Text editor
    • HTML
    • Web – authoring software

    (b) *Any one from:*
    • Digital camera
    • Digital video camera
    • Mobile phone
    • Scanner
    • Web cam

    (c) (i) The file size will be larger than if stored at the lower setting
        (ii) The quality will be improved

    (d) (i) Cropping (or trimming)
        (ii) *Any one from:*
            • Effects
            • Echo
            • Reverb
            • Reverse
            • Adjust volume

    (e) (i) Reduces file size by removing some of the original.
        (ii) *Any one from:*
            • MP3
            • MP4

25. (a) • Fill colour
        • Cropping

    (b) • 640 × 480 = 307200 bits/8 = 38400 bytes
        • 38400/1024 = 37.5 kb

    (c) (i) The number of bits in each pixel used to represent colour
        (ii) Increasing the colour depth increases the file size

    (d) Bit-mapped graphics are resolution dependent.

    (e) *Any one from:*
        • GIF uses lossless compression to reduce file size. JPEG uses lossy compression
        • JPEG uses 24 bits per pixel. GIF uses 8-bit colour code
        • GIF can be animated
        • GIF can be transparent

    (f) Smaller file size

INTERMEDIATE 2 COMPUTING 2011

SECTION I

1. Kilobyte, Megabyte, Terabyte

2. *Any one from:*
    • E-Mail
    • Opening e-mail attachments
    • Opening e-mail messages
    • Using alien disks (Backing Storage)
    • Opening web pages
    • Downloading files from the Internet

3. Registers

4. *Any one from:*
    • Touchpad
    • Trackpad
    • keyboard

5. *Any one from:*
    • Text
    • ASCII
    • RTF

6. 27

7. *Any one from:*
    • Scanner
    • Digital camera
    • Web-Cam
    • Digital Video Camera

8. Technical guide

9. A series of commands or actions are recorded and then these commands can be executed using one keystroke **or**
   Coded using a scripting language and resulting commands executed.

10. Exceptional

11. (a) String

    (b) *Any one from:*
        • Internal commentary
        • White space
        • Modular code
        • Meaningful variable and subprogram names etc

12. volume = height*(length^2) or
    volume = height* length**2

SECTION II

13. (a) *Any one from:*
        • Flowchart
        • Structured diagram

    (b) *Any one from:*
        • The loop must be carried out a fixed number of times (five times, once for each event).
        • A conditional loop would only be used if the number of repetitions is not known in advance.

    (c) *Any one from:*
        Average:=total/events;
        Average:=total/5;

    (d) Array

(e) (i) Incorrect logical operator – should be OR instead of AND

Incorrect relational operator – should be >25 instead of >=25

(ii) Input Validation

(iii) • 5
• 25

(f) *Any one from:*

Allows the user to
• Enter code
• Edit code
• Search and replace
• Format program code eg indentation of structures.

(g) *Any one from:*
• Faster output of multiple copies (ppm)
• Lower running costs

14. (a) (i) 2*3*800*800 = 3840000 bits
3840000/8 = 480000 bytes
480000/1024 = 468.75 kilobytes

(ii) *Any one from:*
Compensates for differences in
• Speed
• Code
• Format
• Voltage
Convert from analogue to digital

(b) *Any one from:*
• Floating point representation
• Mantissa and exponent

(c) (i) Find maximum

(ii) *Any one from:*
• Easier to understand
• Easier to edit
• Easier to find errors
• Portable

(iii) Design

(iv) Compiler translates the whole program into machine code in one operation.

(d) Data Protection Act

15. (a) Object – heading text; operation – font, size of text changed. Object – image: operation – copied, pasted, scaled, rotated, flipped.

(b) *Any one from:*
• Mailing list
• Contact List
• E-Mailing List
• Distribution List

(c) *Any one from:*
• Saving and loading files on disk
• Controls peripherals
• Provides HCI for user
• Manages loading and execution of programs
• Error reporting

(d) (i) *Any one from:*
• Share peripherals eg printers
• Share data
• Share programs (multi-user licence)
• Backup data more effectively
• Control security more effectively
• Communications

(ii) *Any one from:*
• Central store for data and programs that can be accessed by network users
• Automatic backup
• Backups can be easily managed

(e) *Any one from:*
• Detects viruses
• Removes viruses
• Quarantine Files

SECTION III
Part A – ARTIFICIAL INTELLIGENCE

16. (a) *Any one from:*
• Retain knowledge
• Solve problems
• The ability to learn

(b) (i) User communicates with an unseen respondent; if he cannot tell if it is a computer or a person using a computer then it is said to be intelligent.

(ii) *Any one from:*
• No memory of previous conversations
• Uses set keywords to create responses
• Only tests one aspect of intelligence

(iii) *Any one from:*
• Automated translation
• Speech recognition
• Chatterbot
• Natural language database
• Natural language searching

(c) *Any one from:*
• USB flash drive
• Hard disk drive
• CD-R
• CD-RW
• DVD-R
• DVD-RW

17. (a) (i) *Any one from:*
• Computer vision
• Pattern matching
• Vision Systems

(ii) *Any one from:*
• Poor lighting
• Shading from trees
• Weeds very similar to crops
• Weeds growing over crops
• Dirt on lens

(b) (i) Electronic model of the human brain

(ii) *Any one from:*
• Expensive to set up
• Cannot explain reasoning behind how it made its prediction or decision

(c) Evaluation

(d) (i) *Any two from:*
• Expertise always available
• Reduced bill
• Combines expertise of several experts
• Less chance of errors

(ii) *Any one from:*
• Increased processing power
• Increased memory

18. (a) (i) No or false
(ii) X = powershoot

(b) X = fastpics

(c) Match at line 12

Subgoal 1 cost(X,Y)

Match at line 1 X = maxpix, Y = 110

Subgoal 2 Y>200

Subgoal fails

Backtrack to subgoal 1 cost(X,Y)

Match at line 2 X = megashoot, Y = 220

Subgoal 2 Y>200

Subgoal succeeds

(d) free_software (X) if megapixels (X, Y)and Y>10

(e) The search keeps extending down the left hand node downwards until it reaches a solution or backtracks to an earlier success point.

Part B – COMPUTER NETWORKING

19. (a) The mobile phone is only communicating with one other device

(b) Microbrowser

(c) (i) WPAN

(ii) Wireless NIC

(d) *Any one from:*
- To upload music files onto her mp3 player.
- To transfer files between her mobile phone and laptop.
- To update contacts etc.
- To download apps from the www.

20. (a) Implementation

(b) (i) Internet Service Provider

(ii) *Any one from:*
- provide a server space to host the website
- to allow connection to the Internet.
- Provide E-mail access

(c) Uniform Resource Locator

(d) RAM

(e) Hyperlinks

(f) Issue usernames and passwords to the staff

(g) e-sales

(h) *Any one from:*
- To prevent students from accessing inappropriate websites
- To prevent social engineering
- To allow educational sites only.

21. (a) *Any two from:*
- Potential for more sales
- Less staff to employ in future
- Less premises to pay for (rent, electricity etc)
- Wider range of customers

(b) *Any one from:*
- ADSL
- Leased line
- Cable modem

(c) *Any one from:*
- Data is unreadable if intercepted
- For security purposes

(d) *Any two from:*
- Staff could violate confidentiality and protection of customers' data
- Use inappropriate websites during worktime
- Abuse other employees (e-mail bullying) etc

(e) • Hosts names are easier to remember than IP adresses

(f) (i) *Any two from:*
- Data could be lost.
- There may be a fire or flood that could damage data.
- Data could be corrupted in transit etc.

(ii) Any two from:
- Make a backup at least once a day.
- Keep backup tapes in safe place etc.

Part C – MULTIMEDIA TECHNOLOGY

22. (a) Testing

(b) • Flash memory

(c) (i) Crop

(ii) *Any one from:*
- Decrease resolution
- Resampling

(iii) • File size is decreased

(d) *Any one from:*
- Graphics card
- Video graphics card
- Video card

(e) (i) *Any one from:*
- External hard drive
- Flash drive
- DVD-R (not CD-R as lengthy video clips are required to be stored)

(ii) *Any one from:*
- The appropriate software/player is not installed
- Inadequate RAM
- Slower processor
- Incorrect Operating System

(f) (i) *Any one from:*
- Text
- HTML

(ii) *Any one from:*
- He can use the objects already created in his presentation without creating again
- He can see exactly what the web pages will look like to compare to the presentation pages etc.

23. (a) • Sound card (1 mark)
- Microphone (1 mark)

(b) (i) *Any one from:*
- The file size will increase
- Increase the range of values

(ii) *Any one from:*
- Increase the sampling frequency (rate)
- Limit background noise

(c) *Any one from:*
- Effects
- Crop
- Echo
- Tempo
- Volume

(d) *Any one from:*
- Individual notes or instruments can be edited
- No A to D conversion required
- Larger choice of instruments

(e) (i) *Any one from:*
- A digital video camera can have better resolution and/or colour bit depth than a webcam
- More features with digital video camera such as zoom, replay etc
- Digital video camera can store data on tape, DVD etc
- Webcam moved with difficulty/inflexible

(ii) *Any one from:*
- MPEG
- MP4
- WMV

24. (a) *Any one from:*
- Only 2 objects are being used (line and circle)
- There is not enough detail in the graphics to justify pixel level quality
- The logo B is layered

(b) *Any two from:*
- Scaling
- Duplication
- Layering

(c) *Any one from:*
- SVG
- VRML (WRL)

(d) *Any one from:*
- Texture
- Rendering

(e) Bit-mapped graphics produce larger file sizes

(f) Copyright, Designs and Patents Act

INTERMEDIATE 2 COMPUTING 2012

SECTION I

1. Registers

2. *Any one from:*
- Simple two state system where ON is represented by a 1 and OFF is represented by a 0.
- Arithmetic calculations are simpler since there are fewer combinations of 1s and 0s.
- It is easier to represent two states physically on backing storage devices.

3. (a) *Any one from:*
- Via floppy disks
- Homemade CDs
- 'Fun' websites
- E-mail (attachments)
- Sharing infected files

(b) The Computer Misuse Act

4. ROM

5. *Any one from:*
- Falling cost of telecommunication technologies and services
- Shared access to expensive equipment
- Geographical spread of organisations
- Demand for up-to-date information

6. Embedded computer system

7. *Any one from:*
- Communicate
- Analogue to digital (vice-versa)
- Buffering
- Compensates for differences in
  - Speed
  - Code
  - Voltage
  Between the CPU and the peripheral

8. *Any one from:*
- Record user actions (as a series of mouse clicks/moves and assign actions to keystroke)
- Use a scripting language

9. Input validation

10. String

11. *Any one from:*
- Use of meaningful variable names
- Internal commentary
- Using identation
- Use of blank lines (white space)
- Modular code

12. *Any one from:*
- Enter program code
- Edit program code
- Formatting program code

13. Reports mistakes made in the program code as it is being developed.

14. User guide

SECTION II

15. (*a*) The clock speed of the processor (ticks/pulses 2.6 billion times per sec).

(*b*) *Any one from:*
  - More RAM means more data can be stored as Kirsten is working on the laptop.
  - Kirsten can use memory intensive programs (eg video editing) or data (eg high colour bit depth graphics) etc.

(*c*) *Any one from:*
  - Low storage capacity
  - Slower data transfer times
  - Comparison to other drives, eg flash drives, etc, store more data

(*d*) *Any one from:*
  - CD-RW
  - DVD-RW
  - DVD-RAM

(*e*) *Any one from:*
  - Fast printing speeds
  - Dry print outs
  - Larger capacity paper trays
  - Cheaper running costs

(*f*) The list of characters a laptop/device recognises (list of characters on own not enough for mark).

(*g*) *Any one from:*
  - File management
  - Memory management
  - Error reporting
  - Controlling peripherals
  - HCI (GUI)

(*h*) (i) Rich Text Format (RTF)
  (ii) $32 \times 1024 = 32\,768$
  (iii) *Any two from:*
    - Palmtop
    - PDA
    - Smartphone
    - Tablet

16. (*a*) *Any two from:*
  - Mainframes can store large quantities of data
  - Mainframes have high speed data processing
  - Mainframes can multitask
  - Multi-Access

(*b*) Finding the minimum

(*c*) (One dimensional) array

(*d*) *Any one from:*
  - Loop 50 times
  - For 50 countries do

(*e*) *Any one from:*
  (i) • month<1 OR month>12
     • month<=0 OR month>=13
     (One mark for correct month condition, one mark for operator)
  (ii) Conditional

(*f*) (i) *Any one from:*
     1, 01, 12
  (ii) *Any one from:*
    - To ensure the software contains no errors when distributed.
    - To ensure the software is fit for purpose.

17. (*a*) Structure diagram/Chart

(*b*) Implementation

(*c*) *Any two from:*
  - HLLs are written in English like terms
  - Easier to understand
  - Easier to edit
  - Easier to find errors
  - HLLs are problem orientated (not machine)
  - HLLs are portable

(*d*) *Any one from:*
  - Saves time to write the code for the function
  - Can be used many times in different programs
  - Saves time during testing as pre-tested
  - Saves design time as already designed

(*e*) *Any one from:*
  - Program will be easier to understand
  - Program will be easier to change later
  - Original programmer may not be available when changing the code

(*f*) *Any one from:*
  - User needs to know how to install program properly or it won't run
  - User may encounter problems and won't know how to fix them
  - User's computer may not be compatible with program and hence can't be installed

(*g*) (i) *Any one from:*
    - Hyperlink
    - Hotspot
  (ii) *Any one from:*
    - Video files tend to be large and streaming or downloading video data requires a high bit rate.
    - Run more smoothly (not jerky)
    - No buffering
  (iii) *Any one from:*
    - Available 24/7 for sending and receiving mail
    - He can set up mailing lists
    - He can send attachments
    - Faster communication method compared to snail mail etc

SECTION III

Part A – ARTIFICIAL INTELLIGENCE

18. (*a*) *Any two from:*
  - Touch/proximity/pressure
  - Infrared
  - Magnetic
  - Light
  - Sonar
  - Vision (camera)

(*b*) (i) *Any one from:*
    - Speech recognition
    - Language/voice recognition
  (ii) *Any two from:*
    - Background noise
    - Sore throat/cold
    - Slang words
    - Regional/foreign accents
    - Speaking quickly

(*c*) *Any one from:*
  - Computer Vision
  - Vision systems

(*d*) *Any one from:*
  - More memory (RAM)
  - Increased backing storage capacity

19. (*a*) (i) A computer program that mimics the advice of a human expert.
    (ii) *Any two from:*
    - Expertise always available
    - Reduced wage bill
    - Combines expertise of several experts
    - Less chance of errors

(*b*) Chatterbot

(*c*) *Any one from:*
    - Touchscreen
    - Microphone
    - Keyboard

(*d*) (i) Electronic model of the human brain (consisting of many interconnected processors).
    (ii) *Any one from:*
    - Setting up of an artificial neural system is very time-consuming and requires a lot of technical expertise.
    - An artificial neural system cannot explain the reasoning behind how it made its prediction or decision.

20. (*a*) (i) *Any one from:*
    - No
    - False
    (ii) *Any one from:*
    - X=storytelling
    - storytelling

(*b*) as far as the **first** solution.
    Match at line 11
    Subgoal 1 costs(X,Y)
    Match at line 4 X = dance, Y = 3
    1 mark
    Subgoal 2 costs(3>5)
    Subgoal fails
    1 mark
    Backtrack to subgoal costs(X,Y)
    Match at line 5 X = opera, Y = 7
    1 mark
    Subgoal 2 costs(7>5)
    Subgoal succeeds
    X=opera
    1 mark

(*c*) (i)
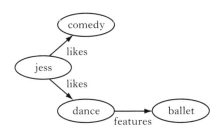
    (ii) Design

(*d*) Breadth-first search

Part B – COMPUTER NETWORKING

21. (*a*) *Any two from:*
    - Services can be available 24/7
    - Has a worldwide customer base so potential for new customers
    - Faster communication with customers
    - Information can be updated quickly

(*b*) File Transfer Protocol (ftp)

(*c*) (i) A browser that is used on small screens of mobile devices.

    (ii) *Any one from:*
    - They have small file sizes which match the small memory sizes of mobile phones.
    - Web-pages can be displayed on smaller screens.

(*d*) Maintenance

(*e*) (i) Hypertext Transfer Protocol (HTTP)
    (ii) The appropriate server is found and translates the domain name into an IP address
    (iii) Running out of domain names.

22. (*a*) Wireless LAN

(*b*) *Any one from:*
    - Wireless Network Interface Card (WNIC)
    - Receiver
    - Transmitter
    - Wireless router

(*c*) *Any one from:*
    - allows portable devices to be used and hence connection can be accessed around the family home
    - less cabling is required therefore less likely to trip over cables

(*d*) *Any one from:*
    - allows connection to the Internet
    - provides e-mail addresses for the family
    - provides appropriate hardware and software

(*e*) Broadband

(*f*) Set up a firewall (filtering software) to filter inappropriate websites and/or keywords.

(*g*) *Any one from:*
    - Use anti-virus software
    - Don't open unknown e-mails or attachments
    - Don't respond to unknown pop-ups

23. (*a*) *Any two from:*
    - Download and upload speeds are too slow
    - One phone line cannot be used for both Internet and phone use
    - Low Bandwidth

(*b*) (i) Leased line
    (ii) *Any two from:*
    - Threats to hardware – (routers, hubs, switches, cables fail etc)
    - Threats to software – (firewalls fail, communication software crashes, network management tools unavailable etc)
    - Denial of service attacks
    - Physical disasters (fire, flood etc)
    - Viruses
    - Hackers

(*c*) Data is changed into a code

(*d*) (i) *Any one from:*
    - Rent on-line movies or sporting events'channels
    - Buy goods
    - Surf the Internet
    (ii) *Any one from:*
    - Smart fridges
    - CCTV or alarm systems
    - Remote heating
    - Remote water sprinklers for the garden
    - Internet access on TV

SECTION II

Part C – MULTIMEDIA TECHNOLOGY

24. (*a*) Analysis

   (*b*) (i) The CCD (charged coupled device) uses sensors to capture light coming in through a lens and then converts it.

     (ii) • 2 gigabytes = 2048 megabytes
        • 2048/2.4 = 853 photographs

    (iii) *Any one from:*
        • Alter brighness
        • Alter contrast

    (iv) *Any one from:*
        • Pixels are removed from the picture
        • Cuts out parts of the graphic that won't be noticed by the human eye.

   (*c*) (i) Description of using a toolbar or dragging and dropping pictures and text frames to create Webpages.

     (ii) *Any one from:*
        • HTML code
        • Text editor

   (*d*) (i) *Any one from:*
        • Digital video camera
        • Digital Camera

     (ii) *Any one from:*
        • AVI
        • MPEG
        • WMV

    (iii) • Increase the frame rate

25. (*a*) (i) Sampling frequency/rate

     (ii) Sampling resolution/depth

    (iii) *Any one from:*
        • MP3
        • MP4

    (iv) (A) *Any one from:*
        • Playing music on a MIDI keyboard
        • Using a MIDI software program to create the music

        (B) MIDI

   (*b*) (i) User can journey through the flat and interact with a computer generated three-dimensional multimedia world.

     (ii) *Any one from:*
        • Data gloves
        • Data suits
        • Virtual reality headset

   (*c*) *Any one from:*
     • Browser
     • File player
     • Viewer

26. (*a*) *Any two from:*
     • Centre
     • Radius
     • Line colour
     • Line thickness
     • Fill colour
     • Layer

   (*b*) *Any one from:*
     • SVG
     • VRML/WRL

   (*c*) *Any two from:*
     • Redrawn to any scale without loss of quality – resolution independence
     • Each object is editable
     • Objects can be grouped

     • Objects can be overlapped without destroying the object underneath
     • Smaller file size than bitmapped graphics which store every pixel

   (*d*) *Any one from:*
     • Graphics Card
     • Graphics Adaptor Card
     • Video Card

Hey! I've done it

© 2012 SQA/Bright Red Publishing Ltd, All Rights Reserved
Published by Bright Red Publishing Ltd, 6 Stafford Street, Edinburgh, EH3 7AU
Tel: 0131 220 5804, Fax: 0131 220 6710, enquiries: sales@brightredpublishing.co.uk,
www.brightredpublishing.co.uk

Official SQA answers to 978-1-84948-269-1
2008-2012